# MEMOIRS OF A MILITANT

# MEMOIRS OF A MILITANT

## MY YEARS IN THE KHIAM WOMEN'S PRISON

BY **NAWAL QASIM BAIDOUN**

EDITED AND WITH AN INTRODUCTION BY **MALEK ABISAAB**
AND **MICHELLE HARTMAN**

TRANSLATED BY **MICHELLE HARTMAN** AND **CALINE NASRALLAH**

OLIVE
BRANCH
PRESS

An imprint of Interlink Publishing Group, Inc.
**www.interlinkbooks.com**

First published in 2022 by

Olive Branch Press
An imprint of Interlink Publishing Group, Inc.
46 Crosby Street, Northampton, MA 01060
www.interlinkbooks.com

Library of Congress Cataloging-in-Publication data:
ISBN-13: 978-1-62371-903-6

Printed and bound in the United States of America

*"In order to carry on with life in prison,
you must believe you will be there forever."*

# — INTRODUCTION —

We first met Nawal Baidoun in the summer of 2018, when the two of us were in Lebanon working on a research project, interviewing women about their stories of the Lebanese Civil War. Nawal Baidoun not only had stories and experiences to relate in her interview, but also a manuscript she had penned during the war. Her handwritten memoirs were preserved on lined paper and written just after her release from the notorious Khiam Prison where she was detained for suspicion of involvement in an Islamic resistance plot to assassinate Israeli collaborator and agent Husayn Abdel-Nabi. Reading Nawal's memoirs reminded us once again how few stories of militant women in the Lebanese Civil War—especially believing Muslim women who participated in armed resistance—have been widely shared. We then endeavored to edit the manuscript, have Nawal herself update it and check it, and publish it in Arabic. But as our project involves a broader scope, we also have translated it into English, to make this story available beyond Lebanon and broader Arabic language readerships. We believe it is inspirational and reveals a great deal, not only about one woman's militant activities, but women's participation in resistance struggles more generally.

## BACKGROUND TO THE PROJECT ON WOMEN IN THE LEBANESE CIVIL WAR

Based at McGill University, our larger project—titled *Women's War Stories: Building an Archive of Women and the Lebanese Civil War*—received Canadian government funding in the form of a grant from the Social Sciences and Humanities Research Council of Canada. A major part of building this archive of stories and histories has been conducting interviews and recording oral histories of women who lived through the Lebanese Civil War. We talked to women with experiences they were ready to relate about their lives in the war, and this has become the basis of a large archive of recordings, which we have begun to study using historical and literary methods of analysis. We are publishing parts of this study in an ongoing way, and post updates on our website: https://womenswarstories.wordpress.com/.

Our ongoing project aspires to collect as many stories as possible related to women's experiences in Lebanon during this war, and its impact on them and their families. Our goal is to make these stories available to audiences in Arabic and English. We hope to share with people the struggles that women faced during the war, and their militancy and resistance especially, because such stories are understudied and so rarely told.

## NAWAL BAIDOUN AND WOMEN IN THE RESISTANCE

The daily lives and social conditions of women during war, and the tools they used to fight for themselves, their families, and/or their country, occupies very little space in prevailing narratives of the history of modern Lebanon. Moreover, women are conspicuously absent from studies that specifically explore the Lebanese Civil War. This is an especially glaring gap when we look at the crucial role they played in the resistance to tyranny and violence in the areas occupied by Israel after the 1982 invasion.

We believe that women's participation was and is crucial to the resistance against occupation and contributed in important ways to its success in South Lebanon. As Nawal Baidoun's memoir makes clear, their roles were not simply limited to offering logistical support to resistance fighters, or providing them with food, clothes, and medical aid, as we usually tend to think. Indeed, women were at the heart of difficult and dangerous missions that required courageous mental and physical effort.

As this memoir demonstrates, Nawal Baidoun's experiences in prison included creative and skillful ways to cope with interrogation and torture, cleverly managing to safeguard the sensitive military and security information that she possessed. She developed the ability to endure both psychological warfare and physical torture by military interrogators. All of this clearly shows Nawal Baidoun's firm convictions, her belief in the justness of her cause, and her willingness to sacrifice her own life for her principles.

Nawal's experience of detention and imprisonment are crucial elements of the memoir you are reading. Her story sheds light on the life of women who were deprived of sunlight, fresh air, decent food, and the pleasure of living with loved ones for years. But these women did still have a life inside prison. Despite constant surveillance by military and civilian prison authorities, imprisoned women found ways to show each other solidarity and sisterly companionship. Their strategies for doing this are inspirational. For example, they brilliantly devised a system for sharing news between different cells in the women's side of the prison and then also between the women's and men's sides. Moreover, they developed a series of signs, symbols, and songs that they used as warnings, alerts, and calls so they could know to be prepared in cases of emergency. The codes and communication network they invented demonstrate the utter failure of the prison authority's attempts to break the women prisoners' resolve, crush their will, and make them feel weak and psychologically defeated.

Their creativity in inventing methods of resistance inside of the prison, and the spiritual and moral connections they constructed with their brothers and comrades across the prison walls, gives the reader an idea about what life was like for women detainees in Khiam Prison. Nawal Baidoun and her comrades were not miserable and sad. In fact, life there defied the misery of prison routines. They remained firm in their hope for victory, throwing off the chains that had oppressed them and defeating their enemy, however long it took.

## THE ASSASSINATION ATTEMPT IN CONTEXT

Nawal Baidoun's memoir opens as she is preparing for a military operation, planning the assassination of an Israeli agent and collaborator in occupied South Lebanon named Husayn Abdel-Nabi, who was eventually killed in 1994.

To give some context, we will provide a brief sense of the historical background and political conditions that prevailed in South Lebanon at this time. In 1976, Israel's occupation army had sponsored the establishment of a proxy army, composed of Lebanese soldiers and officers stationed in Southern Lebanon whom they'd encouraged to defect. This separatist army was called the South Lebanon Army (SLA); its main task was to assist Israeli forces in ruling the occupied Lebanese territories following Israel's first invasion of South Lebanon in 1978. In particular, it was tasked with pursuing and detaining nationalist, leftist, and Islamist cells who had opposed the occupation and launched an armed resistance against them and their Lebanese collaborators. The SLA built a security apparatus that meted out severe forms of abuse and torture to resistance fighters and their families. It spied on anyone who rejected the occupation and its policies, propagating an atmosphere of terror and fear throughout South Lebanon. They destroyed the homes and property of anyone they even suspected of violating their policies.

## WHY WAS HUSAYN ABDEL-NABI THE TARGET?

Husayn Abdel-Nabi was far from the only agent or collaborator in occupied South Lebanon but merely one part of the functioning security apparatus. In addition to him, other prominent symbols include Aql Hashim (executed in 1999) "whose reputation for fear and death precedes him;"[1] Abdel-Nabi Bazzi, also known as Al-Jalbout (executed in 1994); Fawzi Abdel-Karim al-Saghir (executed in 1999); and Joseph Karam, nicknamed 'Aloush (executed in 1999).[2] Another list of operatives known for espionage and terrorism has more recently emerged, including Jawad Zalghout, Faris Abisamra, Ghassan Nahra, and others, most of whom were eventually assassinated.[3]

Husayn Abdel-Nabi was one of the most senior officials in this security apparatus, which spread havoc and terror wherever they went among innocent people living under occupation, not to mention how they encroached on people's lives and properties. Abdel-Nabi was born in 1960 in a village called Bra'ashit, eight kilometers from Bint Jbeil in Southern Lebanon. He spent his childhood in this town, but he and his family were displaced to Hayy Madi in the southern suburbs of Beirut at the beginning of the 1970s. In Hayy Madi, when he was about 15 years old, he started spending time with a group of boys who were drug users and dealers. He spent about four years in this setting, after which he joined a Palestinian organization called the Arab Front for the Liberation of Palestine (AFLP).

But the AFLP didn't provide him with the necessary cover and protection needed when the Burj al-Barajneh bureau of the Lebanese police force learned he was using and dealing drugs to young people. They sent a patrol to arrest him, but he managed to escape from a police raid and slip into another building unnoticed. He didn't evade the eyes of the police for long, however. One police officer found him and they exchanged fire. Abdel-Nabi managed to kill him and escaped to Bra'ashit. At the time,

1   Hassaan Bdeir, "Aql Hashim: To keep his memory alive," 4 February 2000.
2   Jihad Bazzi, "The Islamic Resistance: If you return, we return," 25 May 2007.
3   Amal Izzedin, "Dark Stories in a Brutal Record, the Devils' Agents," 5 June 2000, p. 47.

this village was under the protection of international emergency forces. The youth from the nationalist movement learned that he was wanted by the Lebanese state because he was dealing drugs, so they refused to let him join their ranks. He then took refuge with Ali Abdel-Nabi, also known as Abu Subhi, who had strong ties to Ali Qasim Anany. Anany was working at the time as an operative for Saad Haddad, the head of the South Lebanese Army who lived in Kunin, an Israeli occupied village just four kilometers from Bint Jbeil. He helped Husayn Abdel-Nabi and his mother Naima Anany, the sister of another operative called Nabil Anany, escape to Kunin.

Abdel-Nabi and his companions arrived in Kunin on 4 April 1980. The next day, an Israeli military intelligence officer called Abu Noor came and took them to the Israeli military intelligence center in the old telephone exchange building in Bint Jbeil where they were recruited and signed up. Husayn Abdel-Nabi was thirsting for revenge against his hometown Bra'ashit, which had rejected him because of his reputation and behavior. Under the operative Aql Hashim's leadership, he killed a group of young men from the town. The goal of this operation was for Husayn Abdel-Nabi to prove his loyalty to the occupation army.

They arrived in the central village square and carried out their operation in plain view of the Irish detachment of the UN international emergency forces. The Irish forces appeared to have colluded with them because they didn't prevent them from carrying out their plan and, on the contrary, provided them safe and secure passage into the village. Abdel-Nabi undertook this criminal act with a group of youth from the village who had been spending time at Adib Obeid's house, located only 65 meters away from the international emergency force's headquarters. They hit one house with an Energa bomb and another with seven. Three young men died, Darwish Shihab, Husayn Daher, and Ibrahim Ramadan. More than seven other young men were injured. This attack made Husayn Abdel-Nabi notorious and gave him a reputation for terror. It appears that he was then promoted to an advanced position in the Israelis' and Saad Haddad's security apparatus. Abdel-Nabi was responsible for the obliteration of more than twenty houses in Bra'ashit. His infamy and criminal reputation grew, as did his ability to recruit youth from his hometown who underwent military and security training courses. His taste for murder became so addictive that he even killed people who worked with him.

Similarly, on Ashoura in 1983, he kidnapped a group of young men from the village and handed them over to the Israelis. Following this, a farmer named Husayn Naim Farhat was killed, the communist revolutionary Ibrahim Husayn was arrested and subsequently killed in nearby El Marj, and Ali Hassan Shihab and Ahmed Salameh were also murdered. Abdel-Nabi returned to Bra'ashit during the Israeli invasion in 1982 and began abusing both adults and children, detaining and torturing a number of local people from the village. He supervised these torture sessions himself.[4]

He also extorted things from some families, for example, by asking one of their children to buy him military grade weapons, like a Kalashnikov, and threatening to destroy their house if they didn't. Or he would send one of his agents to inform them that someone in the village of Haris—fourteen kilometers from Bint Jbeil—had military weapons that they wanted to sell for a certain price. Then the person sent by Abdel-Nabi would take the specified amount of money and go to Haris on the pretext of buying this weapon. You can imagine how many times this one weapon was sold—perhaps more than a thousand times. In addition to blackmail and extortion, Abdel-Nabi expelled families with leftist or nationalist allegiances from the village. He blackmailed others who wanted to stay for huge sums of money. He also stole passing cars, forcing their drivers to abandon them. He would take them away and return them only after being paid a certain amount of money that he decided on.

All of these actions made Abdel-Nabi a man both influential and feared. He was able to build up a base of followers who were

4    *Al-Shira'a* magazine reports that Husayn Abdel-Nabi participated in the Sabra and Shatila Massacre that took place on 16 September 1982, as well as the massacre that took place in the southern town of Kurbet Selam. 14 February 2000, p. 17.

either afraid of his power or believed that the enemy would remain in Southern Lebanon forever. Abdel-Nabi's propensity for criminality was unparalleled—he offered something to the enemy that no Israeli could offer his country. If he ever learned that another of Saad Haddad's agents was more devoted to the occupation army than he was, he would not hesitate to have him executed.[5] A great deal of unethical and immoral conduct has been reported about Abdel-Nabi. His record is full of chilling stories. For example, his wife's two sisters reported that he forced their third sister to marry him, and that he was so angry with her one day that he put her in an oven to burn her alive. But she managed to escape and was then transferred to a hospital in Israel where she succumbed to her wounds.[6] He tried to remarry, this time a beautiful young woman from Bra'ashit. But she refused him. He reacted by pulling her through the village streets by her hair and kidnapping her brother, so he would compel her to marry him. And in the end, she was forced to do and bore him a son a short while later. But she later suffered burns to her leg and was admitted to a hospital in Beirut for treatment. She never went back to him after this—she asked for a divorce and he gave it to her.[7]

## JOINING THE ISLAMIC RESISTANCE: NAWAL BAIDOUN'S JOURNEY

This brief account of Husayn Abdel-Nabi's attributes and behaviors gives context to the Islamic resistance movement that Nawal Baidoun joined. The movement tasked her with ridding the people of occupied South Lebanon of him and his evil. Nawal shared with us that one of the main reasons compelling her to talk to us about her experiences in the Islamic resistance is to refute the common and prevailing idea and assumption that most of the key players in the Islamic resistance were and are male youth.

5    Khalil Shihab, Skype interview with the authors, (Montreal-Bra'ashit) 5 June 2020.
6    Amaal 'Izzeddin, "Dark Stories from a Brutal Record", p. 50.
7    Ibid.

Before delving too far into Nawal Baidoun's own path to the resistance struggle, we find it necessary here to offer a brief summary of her early life and how it relates to the nationalist movement—including defending both Palestine and the Lebanese homeland from continual Israeli aggression.

Born in 1924, Nawal Baidoun's father was a member of the Palestine Liberation Organization (Fatah). From childhood, she knew he had a weapon at home, a Browning pistol. It would be lying next to him, and she would fix her eyes on it. She asked her father the reason he had this weapon at home, and he explained to her that it was important to have on hand in case he had to defend the family from Israeli attacks. Nawal was raised with Israel's continual threat to her and her family being very real. She lived in an atmosphere of nationalist resistance. She often listened to conversations between her father's Lebanese and Palestinian nationalist activist friends when they visited.

"I was very aware of this," Nawal reports. Her political evolution developed as a teenager, when she would listen to Palestinian revolutionary songs, like Marcel Khalifeh's nationalist tunes, especially "You are my Enemy, Leave Every House, Neighborhood and Street."

Nawal had one brother who was a martyr for the cause and another who was a prisoner in an Israeli detention center. As she puts it, she was born into a nationalist atmosphere, within a family environment that was always involved in the resistance against Israeli attacks on Lebanon. Nawal's family, which consisted of her mother, father, five brothers, and three sisters was very tight knit. This helped Nawal develop herself as an activist and militant.

## ARREST. DETENTION. AND RELEASE

On the night of her arrest, Nawal mentally went over each of her family members and how she expected they would react when they heard the news. She first thought about her father who was 65 years old, and then her mother. She thought about her younger brothers who might set out to avenge her when they found out what had happened. She hoped they wouldn't, out of fear they would be harmed. She thought about her youngest brother Jihad who was only eleven years old. When she was released, he was fifteen, and she didn't recognize him at first. Nawal expected that her family would be proud of her and she was not disappointed. The first thing her brother Yasser, who had also been in prison, said when he saw her again was, "You made us proud!"

But Nawal did regret one thing, which happened a year and a half after she was arrested—that her brother Jamal was martyred while she was in prison and she was never able to see him in person again. She did, however, see him on the day he was killed—in her dreams—as if he had come to bid her farewell while she was asleep. She dreamed of him in a spot near the cemetery. She saw them open fire and fatally wound him. She awoke from this nightmare screaming out loud, frightening the prison guards who ran into her cell to find out what was happening. Jamal's martyrdom became a recurring dream on the nights that followed, but what Nawal didn't realize was that it had actually happened. Her female comrades who were imprisoned with her learned about his martyrdom from F.Y., a prisoner and informer. But they didn't confirm the news to Nawal out of concern for her morale and psychological well-being. Even Nawal's neighbors and relatives and the people who came to congratulate her on her release didn't tell her about it either. They'd been asked not to because everyone knew how attached she was to her family and how much she loved them.

Nawal asked about him when she saw his wife and son. They replied to her in vague terms, telling her he'd travelled to Germany. But she had many doubts. Later, she became increasingly suspicious. For example, when she was searching for some of her clothes in her mother's closet, she found black mourning clothes hanging there. She thought it was strange and asked her mother why she had them. But out of concern for Nawal, her mother still didn't come clean. Everything stayed like this until the day came—one month after her release—when she was out visiting the family of a friend from prison, Ahlam Awada, in Beirut with her father and brother Amer.

During the visit, Ahlam's mother asked to speak to Nawal alone in another room. Ahlam's mother launched an introductory speech about the Civil War and its horrors. She showed Nawal pictures of her son and daughter who had been martyred during the war. From this she segued into the topic of martyrs who had died in the war, and the meaning of martyrdom more generally. She started telling Nawal that she knew what a good, believing woman Nawal was, and that she knew that Nawal had decided to join the struggle and resistance knowing that on this path you expect to be martyred one day. She finished by emphasizing that Nawal's brother Jamal had chosen the struggle too—he'd belonged to the AMAL movement and risen within its ranks to become an important figure of the resistance. He was martyred in a resistance operation against a patrol by Israel's proxy army the SLA on July 15, 1990. Nawal did not immediately understand what Ahlam's mother was saying to her. She only realized it when she rejoined her father and brother in the living room. She fainted at that moment from the sheer trauma of the shock.

Nawal learned later that her martyred brother, Jamal, had written in his will that he did not want them to hang up his picture as people do of those who sacrifice themselves for the cause. This showed the depth of his belief in the nationalist cause and his willingness to sacrifice his life for it. Nawal's father also believed that this national struggle necessitated sacrifices and that they should not be rewarded with money or material possessions. He refused to receive a stipend the Lebanese State's Council of the South provided to families of arrested or imprisoned women. He did the same when they offered him compensation after Jamal was martyred for the cause. His principles demanded he refuse any trade in his son's blood and sacrifice. He always said, "Only a corrupt person would sell out their own country." Nawal completed his thought herself, in our interview, "A person who sells out their land and principles, sells out completely."

In her memoir, Nawal expresses that people should bear the consequences for the paths they have chosen in life. She described the time
she spent in the Khiam Prison as a rich experience, which tested the
sincerity of her faith and the principles she believed in. She describes
people, from the time of her arrest in the late eighties, as having firm
convictions and commitment to a cause. They believed in its justice and
were prepared to make sacrifices for it.

Nawal was brought up in a family devoted to the nationalist cause,
and her mother was religiously committed. They lived among ordinary
people, men and women who were believing Muslims, brethren in the true
meaning of the word. She recognizes that the popular surroundings of Bint
Jbeil, and her family's house specifically, had a great impact in determining
her political direction and choice to join the struggle. To demonstrate her
family's attachment to nationalist issues and causes rather than sectarian,
identitarian or regional ones, she points to her father's affiliation with the
Palestinian Fatah movement. Nawal was very young when she started
listening to the Voice of Palestine radio show and reading whatever PLO
publications she could find, to support the notion that both nature and
nurture play a fundamental role in forming a person's political consciousness. Nawal notes that her own political consciousness developed through
the influence of the Islamic resistance. This was the main party in Bint
Jbeil after the Israeli invasion of 1982. Hezbollah was weakened and even
the influence of the Fatah movement and the rest of the Palestinian and
Lebanese organizations in the region were flailing.[8]

In the period leading up to the plot to assassinate Husayn Abdel-
Nabi, Nawal was having a difficult time pursuing her law degree at the
University of Saida, the capital of South Lebanon. While studying, she
had to work as a teacher in the Bint Jbeil School so that she could afford
to pay for both university and transportation between Bint Jbeil and
Saida.[9] Like most people living in South Lebanon at the time, her life was
very difficult. She woke in the morning to the sounds of missiles being

8    Nawal Baidoun, interview with the authors in Bint Jbeil, July 2018.
9    Ibid.

launched by Israeli forces against villages and towns in South Lebanon. Her day might turn into hell; violence and murder could interrupt any sense of normalcy, safety, or even survival at any time. Nawal reports how this was a part of daily life in South Lebanon, but that these abuses of ordinary people increased dramatically with the Israeli invasion of Lebanon in the summer of 1982.

Nawal lived under occupation for years, and like everyone else suffered from its cruelty. She became increasingly aware of how necessary it was to build a resistance against the occupying army. Nawal's militant spirit came to life with every strike against the occupation. She began to feel it was her duty to help her sisters and brothers in struggle. So she decided to volunteer for clandestine organizations, at first by collecting information about the movements and positions of the occupation forces and their local operatives. She memorized and retained information, hoping the day would come when it could be used in service of the resistance. Initially, the nationalist resistance actively fought the occupation forces, but as soon as the Islamic resistance began to appear, Nawal grew more enthused about joining the battle to liberate her country.

In the first period of her work with the resistance, from 1984 to 1988, Nawal's activity was limited to facilitating logistical matters, including smuggling and hiding weapons into the occupied areas. There was an escalation of resistance operations in this period, and consequently the occupation forces increased the frequency of arrests and the detention of innocent people, accusing them of violent actions they weren't responsible for. After each action carried out by the resistance, there would be more arrests of militants, activists, and their family members, on the basis of mere suspicion of involvement. This was an intimidation tactic. There was such an enormous increase in arrests that the areas living under the occupation were emptied of young men. Thus, young women started feeling a responsibility to take action and struggle against arbitrary arrests and prevent the occupation from emptying the region of their sons and brothers.

In 1986, occupation forces randomly arrested one of Nawal's brothers, who wasn't even sixteen years old, along with a group of other young people. This was after an armed resistance operation against an occupation position in Bint Jbeil. After his release from prison, there were signs of torture still visible on his body. This was difficult for Nawal to witness and increased her determination to work with the resistance to rid the region of the occupation once and for all. Thus, with women comrades in her town, she began communicating with the young men in the Islamic resistance outside of the occupied area. Nawal grew more and more committed to participating in resistance operations because of her belief, as she put it, "that young women are able to do things... Because we young women weren't being watched as much, we were able to avoid drawing the attention of the occupation forces."[10]

## THE ASSASSINATION PLOT

Nawal's most serious task was to orchestrate the assassination of Husayn Abdel-Nabi. According to her, he "had a notorious reputation for criminal behavior and abuse." The plan that Nawal devised was to carry out the assassination with a silencer pistol. This meant planning, surveilling the target, collecting intelligence about him, weapons training, and then finally implementing the plan. Studying law at the university in Saida, sixty-eight kilometers from Bint Jbeil, made Nawal better able to contact the resistance, train as an operative, and get the weapon she needed. She managed to procure this weapon so secretly that even the other young women who were participating in the operation with her didn't know what kind of gun it was or even that she had taken possession of it. Nawal confirms that this secrecy, even from other members of the group who were participating in the operation, was necessary for its success. The reader of this memoir will notice that secrets—like not letting it

---

10    Nawal Baidoun, interview with the authors (July 2018).

be known she was in possession of the pistol—ended up playing a key role in misleading investigators and protecting resistance operatives. The process of monitoring, tracking, and gathering intel about the target, Husayn Abdel-Nabi, took seven months. A mistake made by one of the participants in the operation, however, led to its ultimate failure and the arrest of the entire group.

This small error turned out to have a significant impact and result. One of Nawal's female comrades made this mistake while she was gathering information about Husayn Abdel-Nabi. The young woman charged with this task lacked experience in clandestine actions and had a "less developed activist consciousness," as Nawal put it. She had a friend from school whose home she used to visit from time to time. By chance this friend was related to Abdel-Nabi. One time, this young operative asked her friend about Husayn Abdel-Nabi. She posed questions about when he would typically come for visits, what kind of car he used, what people were part of his entourage, and how many they were.

This caught her friend's attention and she told Abdel-Nabi that there was a girl at school asking a lot of questions about him. Abdel-Nabi took this very seriously and asked her to keep talking to the girl so he could get a better idea of the purpose of her questions and learn more. Once he had a full picture of the situation, he arrested two young women in the group, with the initials F.Y. and K.Z.[11] This happened on a Wednesday in the month of Ramadan in 1988. Nawal figured that her turn was inevitably coming next, but she didn't expect it to come so quickly. People in Bint Jbeil began spreading the news of F.Y. and K.Z.'s arrest, but Nawal changed nothing about her normal daily routine, and the next day she went to work at school as usual.

After work, she returned home and her two sisters, Ghada and Nadia, noticed that she seemed a bit off. Nadia asked her why and Nawal answered that perhaps she was feeling a bit irritable because of the Ramadan fast. Nawal remained clear-headed, despite the many thoughts

11    Throughout the memoir, identities are protected by referring to people by their initials rather than their full names. MA and MH.

rushing through her mind at the time. She decided that she shouldn't flee town and would stick to the plan. She would simply have to deal with the results and consequences of the decision she'd made.

She knew from the moment she'd joined the resistance that she had to expect to face difficulties, but she didn't want to burden her family or cause them any problems. That same evening when Nawal was reading the Qur'an waiting for the call to prayer to break her fast, she heard knocking at the door. She opened it to find the Israeli agent Husayn Abdel-Nabi accompanied by two other operatives, one of whom—Abdel-Nabi Bazzi, nicknamed Al-Jalbout—was from Bint Jbeil. The other was Fawzi al-Saghir.[12] Husayn Abdel-Nabi asked her right off if she was Nawal Baidoun. She replied in the affirmative and he asked her to come with them to their headquarters for questioning about a serious matter. Nawal asked him to give her a couple of minutes to finish her prayers and change her clothes, but he started immediately swearing, blaspheming, and waving his gun around as if he were going to open fire. Nawal found she had no choice but to ride with them in a military vehicle that drove them to the security forces headquarters in Bint Jbeil.[13]

---

12   Abdel-Nabi Bazzi (Al-Jalbout) was an operative who became responsible for the Beit Yahun crossing after Husayn Abdel-Nabi. Al-Jalbout participated in the kidnapping of citizens and his name was also associated with many instances of torture. He was killed by the resistance in the town of Beit Yahun on 7 March 1994. The operative Fawzi al-Saghir took over the Beit Yahun crossing after Al-Jalbout was assassinated, where he also carried out many kidnappings, as well as torture and abuse. The resistance assassinated him in the summer of 1999. *Al-Shir'a* (14 February 2000: 17-18).

13   Immediately after their occupation of South Lebanon, the Israelis established a basic security center at the telephone exchange in Bint Jbeil, which belonged to the Lebanese state government and was called the "Centrale." Khalil Shihab, who was arrested by the Israelis in 1982, recounts that the security center at the Centrale was supervised by a senior Israeli security officer called Abu Noor and a Major General called Ghadi. Shihab says that Ghadi interrogated him after Husayn Abdel-Nabi, accompanied by an Israeli patrol, arrested him on 9 July 1982 in Bra'shit. Shihab was charged with carrying a weapon of war, but he denied the charge. The Israeli interrogator showed him an old photograph of himself carrying a "Degtyarov" submachine gun in his town and added another charge to the first one: attacking the Israeli army. The Israeli interrogator ordered Shihab be transferred to the center for military governance in Sour, which was destroyed by the resistance on 11 December 1982. From there he was transferred to Ansar Prison where he was detained for thirteen months. Shihab

## KHIAM PRISON, TORTURE AND INTERROGATION

Abdel-Nabi himself began Nawal's interrogation. She was subjected to all kinds of torture, along with the constant threat of being raped.[14] The interrogators used psychological and physical torture. They forced her to listen to obscene language about what they would do to break the will of a religious woman like her; they ripped off her hijab and wiped their dirty shoes with it. They put a bag over her head so she couldn't see their faces—meaning that, despite their power and authority, they were afraid she would recognize them and expose their identities. They then began Nawal's physical torture, using different methods, including electric shocks and pouring cold water over her.

Despite harsh and violent torture, Nawal never changed her answer to their questions: "I don't know." She was so convincing that they suspected that they might have had the wrong person or that there was perhaps another Nawal Baidoun out there. Nawal maintained her composure and didn't give up anything until the other young women from her cell began to confess things and reveal secret information and intelligence. When the interrogators confronted her with certain bits of information, Nawal began confessing to only things that her comrades, F.Y. and K.Z., had already told them. She confessed to small and unimportant things like how they sent and received encrypted information through the packaging on loaves of bread. She did not, however, confess to the most important thing raised in this investigation—how she had gotten the pistol.

One thing that helped Nawal here is that none of the other operatives or women in prison mentioned the gun under interrogation because they

---

was released on 15 August 1983, but Husayn Abdel-Nabi and the Israelis expelled him from Bra'shit and exiled him to Beirut. Khalil Shihab, interview with the authors.

14   In an interview with the authors, Nawal Baidoun asserts that the verbal threat of rape was intended to intimidate female prisoners to crush their will to resist, force them to surrender, and give up information they were hiding. In fact, as she relates, these prison workers did not dare rape the female prisoners—not because of their good morals and dignity, but out of fear of people's reaction and public opinion. Most important according to her was that they were afraid of reprisals by the resistance. Nawal Baidoun, interview (July 2018).

actually didn't know anything about it, including where it was hidden. Nawal's interrogators also used psychological torture against her, which was very painful especially when they told her that they had detained her younger sister Nadia and demanded that she confess, promising to release her if she did. Despite this, Nawal didn't break under pressure or surrender to their demands. She realized that these were empty threats. Nawal asserts here that the prisoner who justifies giving in under torture and confessing everything they know because its horror has made them weak is a liar. To her, it is only the love of family that can truly affect a detainee and make them give in.[15]

Nawal expresses in the memoir that after her interrogation she felt she had begun a new life. All she had to do was adapt to this new lifestyle in prison. As she puts it, "I was created in that place, and I might have died there. I didn't know if or when I would be released." She carries on discussing this, saying that you must keep on living and convince yourself that you will be detained in prison forever. This is how Nawal lived in Khiam Prison. She got used to the prison routines, survived physical torture and the anxiety that she sometimes felt when the col- laborators and agents would arrest someone who knew something about her work. For example, someone would be arrested who knew details about the military operation that she was supposed to carry out, or one of her female comrades imprisoned with her would suddenly confess to something new. That's when the prison authorities would reopen her case and start interrogating and torturing her again.[16]

---

15   Nawal Baidoun, interview with the authors (July 2018).

16   In 1933, the French occupation authorities established a military barracks in the town of Khiam, which the Lebanese army took over when the French left Lebanon in 1946. In 1978, the Khiam barracks fell into the hands of the South Lebanon Army militia when Israeli forces invaded South Lebanon. They transformed them into an interrogation center, whereas pris- oners were sent to the Ansar compound. When it closed in 1985, the same year the military prison in Artit was emptied of its prisoners, the Khiam barracks were converted into a prison. The prison authorities were divided into two groups. The first was the Israeli administration which included 27 soldiers, officers, and military men who were regularly present at the facility both at fixed times and whenever else the need arose. The second group was composed of South Lebanon Army militia collaborators and agents, and included in its ranks dozens of people who dealt with logistical affairs of the prison—guards, people taking care of communication,

This happened to Nawal about a year and a half after she was arrested, when her comrade F.Y. confessed to some information she'd remembered and told the prison authorities. Then they reinterrogated Nawal. Unfortunately, Nawal tells us, there are detainees who grow weak under torture or who simply can't handle harsh prison life and crumble, turning into what are called "inside informers." In her opinion, these inside informers are even more dangerous than the interrogators because they are able to obtain more precise information from their cellmates than the interrogators can, albeit by different methods. Though the "inside informers" do not use torture like the interrogators do, they are no less dangerous.

## LIBERATION

Nawal was released from Khiam Prison through a prisoner exchange deal brokered by the resistance movement and Germany, who played the role of mediator. This was the same deal on December 1, 1991 which resulted in the release of the kidnapped American hostages Terry Anderson and Terry Waite. They were released in exchange for one hundred and twenty-five prisoners in Khiam and other prisons. The exchange process took place in three parts. Nawal was released in the second batch, which included twenty-five prisoners and the bodies of 100 martyred fighters. Nawal left prison strong and determined to be a voice for all women

security, food, clothing, and fuel—also interrogators, medical staff including two nurses, and finally the five female guards who worked in the women's section. Another group working for the prison authorities were a group called "inside informers" who the prisoners called "Smurfs." They'd been arrested for some reason or other but gave in under torture and offered themselves to the service of the prison authorities for free, by spying on their imprisoned former comrades. They did this in exchange for some measly privileges. It should be noted that the Khiam prison was not subject to any international oversight or international human rights associations. This meant that there was no way to transmit news or write reports to inform the world about the torture and abuse suffered by male and female prisoners, not to mention their appalling health and living conditions. For further explanations of the Khiam Prison and its history see, *The Liberated Prisoner*. Muhammad Ahmad Khishish, *Khiam Prison: Barzakh al-Hayat* (Beirut: Dar al-Walaa, 2014) 12-19.

and men still languishing in Israeli prisons and detention centers. She remained stubbornly persistent in this struggle, devoting every possible effort to completely freeing all remaining prisoners and detainees.

Nawal is proud of what she has done. She affirms that if we were to go back in time to the early days of the struggle against the occupation, there is no doubt in her mind that she would have done it again—she would resist the occupation with every ounce of determination she possesses.

After her release, Nawal took some time to recuperate, joining the remaining members of her family who had been displaced from Bint Jbeil to the liberated zone. She decided to complete her studies in Law at the Lebanese University in Saida. Nawal and the Prisoners' Association also fought hard against the media blackout on the issue of prisoners and detainees in Israeli prisons and detention centers by contacting and meeting with Lebanese government officials, at even the highest levels, in order to make the voices of prisoners heard. They worked hard to communicate the suffering of prisoners to those in power. They urged these politicians to act and put pressure on the international community to force Israel to improve the conditions of prisoners and detainees, including ensuring a path to their release. In this context, Nawal partici-pated in a Hezbollah-supported delegation of the Prisoners' Committee to meet and deliver a protest note to the UN Secretary General Kofi Annan, who was in this position from 1997–2006.

From that time on, the issue of prisoners became more widely known. Their cause and struggle started to be mentioned in the media throughout the world. Similarly, Nawal and the committee visited the Vatican for an audience with Pope John Paul II (who served from 1978–2005) in September 2000. This was a very successful visit. Nawal reports that in her work with the Islamic resistance she didn't experience any untoward or discriminatory behavior toward her as a woman, by her male comrades. When she helped found the Prisoners' Association, she had no problems with the male members with whom she worked in pursuit of a common goal—fighting for the liberation of all prisoners and detainees.

Nawal speaks beautifully about her comrades who welcomed her inside the prison and helped her withstand the harsh and difficult life they shared. They showed each other the heights sisterly solidarity can reach. This left a huge impression on her and had an impact on her political and activist consciousness. Nawal particularly mentions fellow prisoner Sanaa Ali Ahmad who was like a sister who embraced her when she was traumatized, a comrade who bolstered her when she felt weak, and a friend who comforted her when she was sad. Sanaa was a model of resistance and resilience. She defended all the imprisoned women and challenged the arrogance and abusiveness of the male and female prison authorities. She even challenged the interrogators and the prison warden. She was taken to solitary confinement many times for defending her imprisoned comrades, and more than once was held there for defending Nawal. She was never silent when she needed to speak the truth. She was truly a hero in action.

We asked Nawal Baidoun how she withstood the torture she was subjected to in her interrogations, and where she found such resilience when confronted by her interrogators. It's surprising how she was able to keep her secrets without divulging anything, given the brutality she experienced at their hands. The incorrect but prevailing notion is that women are less able to withstand physical torture than men—they are quicker to fold and give the interrogators the information they seek. But Nawal Baidoun's memoir refutes these notions that are biased in favor of men. What sets her experience of resisting torture and preserving her own psychological and mental wellbeing apart is that she not only had the physical ability to resist her torturers and withstand their beatings and electric shocks to her body, but was also extremely intelligent in the way she organized the information she knew about the details of operations. This meant that she could carefully choose what to reveal and what to hide from her enemy.

Was this a result of the security and technical training that Nawal received? Nawal confirms that she did undergo very general training, but it did not go much beyond preparing a detainee on how to confront an interrogator. The aim of the training was to psychologically prepare those engaged in direct actions—so that they would know what to do if they were subject to arrest and had to face an interrogator who would accuse them of many things. She was also told that, if arrested, she could be exposed to brutal torture and enormous psychological pressures. Interrogators could even use a lie detector machine on her. Nawal was thus somewhat prepared to face her interrogators, but she admits here that she was not really ready to deal with an inside informer and did not know how to cope with that. The experiences of female prisoners before her helped her a great deal in this regard. The other women prisoners took her under their wing and always alerted her to things to watch out for, until she built up enough awareness and had sufficient information about how to deal with such situations. Later, she herself was able to do the same for new prisoners. Nawal here points to an important issue, which is that psychological preparation and training about interrogators and interrogations, given by the resistance movements, was not as developed at the time of her arrest as it is now.

This introduction is meant to give the reader a general orientation, background, and context for the time, place, and players in South Lebanon during the Israeli occupation and resistance to it. This memoir provides a first-hand account told from Nawal Baidoun's perspective not long after her release from prison. Her direct and unflinching report of her time in Khiam Prison contains lessons and reminders to us all about not only the cruelty of occupation and imprisonment, but also the human spirit and will to resist. Nawal Baidoun could not rest while her comrades were still in prison. Her message of prison abolition is one that resonates today as we finish writing this introduction—none of us are free until all of us are free.

Malek Abisaab and Michelle Hartman
Montreal, 2020

# — THE MEMOIR —

Nawal Baidoun

## BEFORE PRISON

In late 1986, my village, Bint Jbeil, like all other towns and villages in South Lebanon occupied by the Israeli enemy, was rife with darkness and deprivation, sorrow and misery.[1] Similarly to the rest of the occupied South, Bint Jbeil was continually ravaged by waves of relentless, merciless terrorism. Each day, the Israeli State and its Lebanese collaborators tightened the noose around the necks of the people in these villages in any and every way they could. This included mass arrests of anyone they suspected of having ties to the resistance, or even of people who frequented places of worship. They also increased taxation on raw materials and other commodities that some merchants managed to bring into the region by obtaining specific permits to cross over from outside the occupied zone.[2] On top of all of this, there was the forced

---

1   The town of Bint Jbeil is located in the district of the same name in the larger administrative region of Nabatiya in South Lebanon. It is 67 kilometers away from Saida, the capital of South Lebanon. MA and MH.

2   The exact areas that were occupied changed over time, because the Israeli occupying forces were made to withdraw from some regions by the resistance operations. These resistance operations started from the time of the invasion in 1982 onward. The first withdrawal from Beirut was at the end of September 1982. Then there was a second withdrawal from Mount Lebanon and Kharroub in late September 1983. The third withdrawal happened in June 1985 when the occupying army evacuated Saida, Sour, and Nabatiya. The Israeli Army continued occupying what was then called the "security belt," which included the town of Naqoura and the districts of Marjayoun, Bint Jbeil, and Hasbaya. They withdrew from these areas on 23 May 2000, which is now referred to as the fourth withdrawal. Israel still occupies Lebanese land, in Shebaa Farms, Kfarchouba, and the village of Ghajar. MA and MH.

military recruitment of every boy who had reached thirteen years of age to contend with. If families refused, they would find themselves faced with two options—condemn their sons to jail or banish them from home, to go live outside the occupied areas.

It wasn't safe anywhere, neither on the streets nor at home. No one could ever relax. Someone might even jump out of bed late at night, all aquiver, because of a terrifying pounding on the door: it would be the collaborators, ordering the owner of the house to hurry up and open the door. The collaborators would regularly head to a specific address because they were on the prowl for one of the members of the family living there. And this is how it came to be that in our town, as in so many others, it was difficult to find even one household without at least one family member in prison. Further, any person who so much as grumbled or muttered something that Israeli collaborators might find suspicious would simply be picked up and locked away. This is how Khiam Prison and others filled with hundreds of innocent victims— righteous people. The prison became a cemetery. The Israelis and their local collaborators made it into something whose name alone still has the power to strike fear in anyone who hears it. As the saying goes, "He who enters is lost, but he who comes out is reborn."

Despite all this harassment and abuse, many young people in town still managed to find ways to secretly work with the resistance against the occupation.

In that period, I, like many others, rejected the humiliation of occupation; we preferred death to living in the shadow of this ruthless, merciless brutality. This became all the more pronounced when I saw the young people of my town being subjected to cruel punishments and oppression that I had no hand in stopping. Then a crisis struck the entire town. It was the very beginning of the month of Ramadan in 1986. The Israeli occupation forces, with the help of their local collaborators, began raiding houses in the village, arresting dozens of local young people, and demolishing several homes. The demolitions particularly targeted the neighborhood I was living in, and this disaster sparked a thirst for revenge inside me and many of my peers. No household in our neighborhood was spared; at least one person was arrested and detained from each home. Sorrow and depression sunk into the place and their telltale signs were etched onto the faces of the youth that remained. But inside each of us lay a volcano just waiting to erupt.

The atrocities committed by the occupying Israeli army and its local collaborators continued, and only a few months later a similar incident resulted in the arrest of my brother, who was barely fifteen years old, along with a number of his peers and comrades. There had been an attack on the local Israeli collaborating agents' headquarters, located in the former central telephone exchange office. The same office where they once issued travel permits. The arrests were in retaliation for this operation. As usual, they raided the homes of people living nearby and arrested all of the young men who remained.

## THE WORK BEGINS

Every village in occupied South Lebanon had a local security official. They were all in competition for who could be the most cruel, brutal, and criminal, and who would issue the most severe orders and restrictions against the locals. The security official in my village was the Israeli State's cruelest and most brutal and criminal local agent of all. His name was Husayn Abdel-Nabi. Everyone in the occupied South knew who he was. No one in South Lebanon has not heard his name—in fact, there's no one from the entire region who doesn't know about his criminal actions and abuses against defenseless locals. I had long fantasized about killing this traitor, Husayn Abdel-Nabi, who betrayed his homeland and his own people. This would be our only salvation from his evil. I needed a plan and the means to make my fantasy come true, though I realized that implementing it might mean my own martyrdom.

The year was 1987. At the time I was living with my younger siblings in Bint Jbeil and working as a teacher in a private school in town. The school's location allowed me to monitor local collaborators and Israeli patrol movements, because it stood at the crossroads of three villages: Bint Jbeil, Ainata, and Aitaroun. My sisters and brothers were studying in the village school. But my mother and father had to live outside the occupied zone with my older brothers who had been denied access to our town. Only my mother was permitted to travel into the occupied zone from time to time, to check on us and spend some time with us.[3]

Circumstance would have it that I met another young woman from Bint Jbeil who was also suffering from the hardship of the occupation. Two of her brothers had been arrested and thrown into Khiam Prison in 1986. We weren't very close friends before this, but we soon started to meet more frequently. Every time we got together, we would have long conversations about the youth who had been arrested and detained, especially the young men of our neighborhood—we were like sisters to them, and I'd been aware of most of the actions they were taking against the occupiers. Over the course of these conversations, it became clear to me that this woman harbored a desire for revenge no less intense than my own.

I'm not the only one who noticed this about her. It was generally accepted in Bint Jbeil that she fiercely hated the occupiers and their local collaborators and agents. So, we continued our meetings until I could be certain that we—together with other young women like us—could take action against them. We couldn't just stand idly by and do nothing. There was a young woman in our group who was among the first to show her willingness to take action against the Israelis and local collaborators. She was extremely religiously devout and committed to her faith. Her brothers were among the first to be thrown into the Khiam Prison in 1986. This alone was enough to fuel her desire for retaliation and push

---

3    In my family, I am the eldest of five boys and three girls. My brothers lived with my parents outside Bint Jbeil, where they were exiled because of their role in the resistance. Before the Israeli invasion and occupation of South Lebanon in 1978, my father owned a shoe factory, but the Israelis completely demolished it when they occupied Bint Jbeil. My father was then forced to leave the city because of his involvement with the PLO at the time—as it was the resistance movement against the Israelis. NB.

her to join the resistance to avenge them.

During this period, I was permanently glued to the news, mostly the radio, for security reports and updates. I used to especially listen for any stories about resistance operations against the enemy occupiers and their collaborators. I also listened to patriotic and revolutionary songs, including Palestinian anthems like, "Be on Guard my Enemy." These were the kinds of songs that stirred up passion and energy in the hearts of all free citizens.

For a long time—I would say about a year and a half—my friend and I worked together to monitor the movements of Israeli occupying patrols. Then the scope of our work expanded. We began supplying our friends in the resistance outside Bint Jbeil with important, thoroughly vetted information, useful to carrying out military operations. We would send this information secretly, hidden inside loaves of flat pita bread for example. Things continued like this, and our brothers in the resistance outside the occupied area were able to carry out many successful operations based on the information we'd provided.

## PLANNING THE OPERATION

In addition to what I was already doing—collecting information and hiding small arms—my every thought was focused on undertaking one specific task. If I managed to complete it, I would deal a powerful blow to the Israeli occupiers and their collaborators and thereby liberate the people who had been subjected to the evils of a mass murderer. This murderer was the traitor Husayn Abdel-Nabi, whom we used to call Husayn Enemy-Nabi, playing on the sounds of his last name.[4]

The crucial and central issue was how to get the equipment we needed to implement the operation—a pistol and a silencer—into our

---

4    This is a play on words between the original name and its meaning, Abdel-Nabi—Servant of the Prophet. In Arabic, the word Abdel- was replaced with Aduw-el- (which sounds similar in Arabic)—meaning "enemy of." Thus, the name "Enemy-Nabi" means Enemy of the Prophet. The play on words is intended to convey how evil Abdel-Nabi was. CN and MH.

town, which was located within the occupied zone. But I also underwent weapons training with a fellow member of the resistance outside this zone. I learned how to do many things, including how to assemble and disassemble weapons. In addition to this, I learned about the strategy and implementation of such operations.

My female comrades and I began setting our plan in motion. At first, this involved monitoring the movements of our target, the places he frequented, the companions he spent time with, and the kinds of vehicles they moved around in. The principal obstacle standing in our way was: how to get the gun and silencer into Bint Jbeil. It wouldn't be easy. Even though we travelled back and forth between Bint Jbeil and areas outside the occupied zone—we all had either family or work commitments on the outside—it would be no easy feat for one of us to carry it back.

One of my girlfriends K.Z. often went to the village of Tebnine, where she was studying to become a staff nurse.[5] As for me, I often travelled to the area near Bint Jbeil where my family was living and to Saida, where I was pursuing my university studies. During 1988, I was finishing my second year of Law School. Each of us tried to secure the weapon we needed from the places we visited. Until we were able to develop a plan to bring it in, we continued to monitor our target and his movements, collecting every bit of information we could on him, no matter how small. In the end, I managed to smuggle the gun in with the help of my comrade who had trained me. I'd disassembled it first, to make it easier to hide.

But then the Israeli collaborators took us by surprise—it was the kind of moment that we had always discussed in our conversations and at our meetings. On April 19, 1988, a Wednesday afternoon to be exact, the target Husayn Abdel-Nabi and two of his agents—Abdel-Nabi Bazzi, nicknamed Al-Jalbout, and Fawzi al-Saghir, both from Bint Jbeil—arrested K.Z. at her place of study in town. They also arrested F.Y. at her home. A strange feeling I'd never experienced before washed

---

5   The town of Tebnine is located in the Bint Jbeil district, about 12 kilometers from the town of Bint Jbeil. MA and MH.

over me, but I didn't do anything or react in any way that showed I was worried, or even that I knew either one of them.

Time passed slowly. All day, the only thing I could think about was getting home, but I had to wait for the final bell to ring. I finally returned home, thinking about what had happened to my comrades and what would happen to me. My siblings, who were already there, noticed that something was bothering me. But I insisted that nothing was going on and that I was perfectly fine. The whole time, I kept thinking about what had happened and what would follow—how and why had the two of them gotten arrested? Had the local Israeli collaborators figured out what we were up to? Would K.Z. and F.Y. be released if nothing was found? Or would I end up joining them? So many questions were swirling around in my head. The following day, I went to school and kept up appearances. I was surprised that the teaching staff had heard news of the arrests and were all outraged.

One of the women workers at the school said: "The people of the village should all stand together against this, religious clerics should condemn these arrests, there should be a sit-in at the town square. Has the world gone mad? Has it come to this, locking up the girls in town? And why? They've taken all the boys, so now they're coming for the girls!" These words, which she voiced out loud with no reservations, still resonate with me today. This working woman had a political position that not one of my colleagues on the teaching staff would dare show openly at school.

Somehow the school day ended, and I managed to make my way back home. The incident had paralyzed me, but I tried to act completely normally for fear that my siblings might notice something. Then my time was up: the moment I had been waiting for arrived—that is, the moment of my arrest.

It happened at six fifteen in the evening, on Thursday, April 20, 1988—the fifth day of Ramadan. I was busy preparing for the iftar. Just five minutes before the breaking of the fast, I heard wild knocking on the door to the house. I could feel my heart beating stronger and faster than the pounding at the door. I hurried to see who was there, and I was shocked to find three collaborators with the Israeli occupying army standing there: Husayn Abdel-Nabi, aka Enemy-Nabi, Kamal Salih, from Ayta al-Shaab, and Fawzi al-Saghir, from my own town, Bint Jbeil.

I asked them, "What is it? What do you want? There is no one here but my brother who is not even thirteen years old, and my two sisters, younger than me." It seemed that my turn had come. Husayn Abdel-Nabi just looked down at his hand and said to me, "Are you Nawal Qasim Baidoun?"

"Yes," I replied, "What do you want?" It turns out that my name was written on the palm of his hand.

"Come with us to town, we'd like to ask you some questions. It won't take long and then you can come back home," he told me.

"What do you want from me? What do you want to ask me about?"

"Come with us, you will soon know everything there is to know."

At this point, Fawzi al-Saghir interrupted saying, "We would like to clarify a few things with you, it will only take five minutes. Don't worry. This may all turn out to be a simple misunderstanding."

But this was neither a misunderstanding, nor would it take five minutes. Wasn't this what they always said, though it typically led to years of detention in an Israeli prison? I insisted on knowing why I was being taken into town and said that I wouldn't go with them unless they told me the reason why. And then the infamous Husayn Abdel-Nabi waved his gun in my face and threatened loudly, with a vengeful tone, "You'll come with us or I'll shoot you."

By then, all the neighbors had gathered around. I tried to make out where my siblings were. Just a moment ago, they'd been right next to me helping prepare the iftar, but now I couldn't see any of them. Perhaps they were still nearby, but I couldn't spot where they were. At that very second when the Israeli agent aimed his gun at me, threatening to shoot, one of my neighbors—the mother of a prisoner who had been detained by the Israelis for a year and a half—motioned at me to stay silent. I smiled weakly at her. Then I asked them to give me time to pray and change my clothes. This made Abdel-Nabi even angrier and he brandished his gun, holding it closer to my face. That movement was accompanied by a screech from the same neighbor, frightening everyone around me, "Enough! Stay quiet!"

I smiled at her again, in farewell, and walked away with them.

The place we were heading to was the old central telephone exchange office. It was about a ten-minute walk from our house, perhaps a little bit more. As we were walking, I noticed a number of other neighbors who lived a bit further from our house peering out at us. They had already heard the news. How, I have no idea. I looked at them with a smile that held a thousand meanings. Fear was visible on their faces, or perhaps it was pity for me and the situation I'd ended up in. We arrived at our destination as it was growing dark, the sounds of the muezzins' voices calling out the Ramadan prayers.

When we arrived, they hurried me inside. One of the guards there ordered me to step forward and opened a door. Husayn Enemy-Nabi pushed me inside a door that led to a room. In the corner, there was a metal cupboard, across from a table. He led me over to the table and sat me down on a metal chair. He sat down on the other side. His other two agents, Kamal Salih and Abdel-Nabi Bazzi nicknamed Al-Jalbout, remained standing. Al-Jalbout seemed to have been waiting at the center while the rest of them had gone to collect me from my house. The third agent, Fawzi al-Saghir, stood outside the door to the room.

Enemy-Nabi ordered the guard to lock the door and asked me directly, "Do you live in town full time?" I replied, "Pretty much, yes. I only leave to visit my parents and go to university."

He continued, "I don't see you around town, but I've learned that you're a teacher. What do you teach? Religion?"

His tone implied that he regarded the teaching of religion as a means of resistance, a weapon to be used against them.

No sooner had I replied, "I teach languages," than he fired back, "What's your relationship to K.Z. and F.Y.?" He was referring to the two young women who had been locked up the day before.

"I hardly know them at all. I just know they're other women my age in town." Then he carried on asking me in a very loud voice where I'd hidden the weapons and equipment. "I don't know anything about any equipment or any weapons," I answered.

He asked me directly, "Do you know where K.Z. and F.Y. are?" I feigned ignorance and said, "I don't know, why are you asking me about them?"

He told me they were now in Khiam, without referring to it as a prison, and then stated, "If you don't confess, you'll follow them," carrying on with, "F.Y. says that you have equipment, secret codes, and weapons with silencers. Confess everything, tell us where they are, and we'll release you immediately. You seem clever enough. Don't spoil your future. You're better off confessing."

"I don't know what you're talking about. I know nothing about that woman or any others."

"Is there anyone else in Bint Jbeil with the same first name or family name as you? Is there anyone else with the same exact name as you who F.Y.'s confession might be about?" he taunted. But I kept my composure. He called me again by name, "Nawal Baidoun, you have two choices: either you confess to everything and I let you go home, or I send you to Khiam—no doubt you've heard of it? You're better off confessing, come on. Where did you hide the equipment and the weapons?"

"I don't know what you're talking about…" I told him. He cut me off angrily, "It seems as though a soft touch doesn't work with you. Look on top of the cupboard, do you know what that is?" By taking just a quick glance at it, I could tell that it was a machine used for torture by electric shock. It was a black square box in the shape of an old-fashioned telephone. But I pretended not to know what it was.

He continued talking, "You're going to get to know it now. It's an electrical device. Let's try it out and maybe then you'll change your tune." He put the machine on the table and unraveled electric wires from the sides. He told me to lay my hands on the table. I did. He took one of the wires and wrapped it around the fingers of my right hand, then took the other wire and wrapped it around the fingers of my left. He stood back for a moment and said: "One last chance, will you confess or not?"

"I told you already. I don't know anything, and I don't know anyone."

All it took was a nod of the head and the so-called Al-Jalbout quickly stuffed a gag in my mouth. Then he himself turned the key in the machine. I felt my body jump off the ground. It almost stopped my heart. Then he cut off the current for a moment. "That's nothing. I'll start all over again and I won't stop until you signal with a nod of the head that you're ready to confess. You'll let me know, won't you?"

He continued torturing me with electric shocks, this time using a stronger current than the time before. I felt that my soul was being ripped from my body. I nodded my head to stop the torture. He paused, and then sat down on the chair behind the table to resume his "soft touch." He started off by advising me that even if I could survive this torture, it was nothing—nothing compared to the torment I would find in Khiam. I'd be better off, he said, simply to confess. I was already aware of the methods of torture they used there in the prison, and that they included electric shocks.[6]

He was laying my options out before me, while I was looking down at my hands, tied up with electrical wires. Suddenly an idea flashed through my head and I knew I could translate it into action. I could start to unravel one of the two wires binding my hands without him seeing. I looked at him as he continued to counsel me to confess. "I will ask you one last time, where did you put the weapon and equipment?"

---

6    The methods of torture in Khiam Prison varied. The most common methods used were: electric shocks, beatings with electrical wires, hanging on an electricity pole, sleep deprivation, withholding food and medical attention, sensory deprivation (with a bag over the head for example), being shackled, solitary confinement, confinement in very small spaces, insults and threats, threatening the torture of relatives. Women specifically were threatened with sexual assault or with having their hijabs removed publicly. Male and female prisoners also experienced a kind of collective punishment by being forbidden to wash and being forbidden for days from emptying their waste, which they had to collect in buckets in cells, such that they were forced to live with filth and stench for days at a time. The prison authorities used food to break the will of the prisoners by reducing the amount of food they were given, thus making them unable to think about anything other than how they would "get their next meal," as one of the prisoners put it, rather than about freedom. More detail is available in the publication on the *Al-Ahrar Prison* published by the Lebanese Association for Prisoners, 142. MA and MH.

My response was, "I told you, I don't know anything. I don't know about any equipment or any weapon." He didn't even wait for me to finish speaking before he turned the machine on once again. He was genuinely shocked when I didn't even twitch, despite the fact that he'd amped up the current. He rose up over the table to look at my hands. He discovered that I had pulled one of them free. He roared with anger. Curses and obscenities rained down upon me, and he said that this would be the end of me. In a voice so loud, you could hear it at the other end of the building, he ordered me to put my hands back out on the table and not move them. At that moment, Al-Jalbout and Kamal Salih, who was later killed by his colleagues in a drug raid, stood next to me.

With a swift cruel motion, Enemy-Nabi retied the wires tightly around my fingers. He turned the torture machine to high, and one of the others put the gag back in my mouth. For a few moments I felt that my heart had stopped beating and that I could almost touch the ceiling, because the current was so strong. I don't remember what happened after that; I only remember waking up on the ground with water being poured over my face. He ordered me to stand up. After trying to for a few moments, I finally managed to stand up with great effort. I felt a cold liquid seeping from my head that I assumed was water. I touched it and when I looked at my hands, I realized that it was blood oozing from my head. I must have hit something when I fell. It didn't hurt at all at first, but then later it ached terribly. It was only then that I realized that it was from the impact of my fall.

Enemy-Nabi stared at me and said, "No one on earth attempts to trick me and lives to tell the tale. I will have them take you to Khiam and keep you there forever. I'll personally supervise your torture. I'll teach you to trick me." Then he turned to Al-Jalbout and said, "Tomorrow morning transfer her to Khiam. For now, put her in the room inside, shut the door, and lock it. Don't let anyone from her family in to see her." Then he turned his back and left. As he was walking out, I heard him tell Fawzi al-Saghir the same thing he'd told Al-Jalbout about transferring me to Khiam the following morning.

Al-Jalbout and the guard did what he'd ordered them to do. They deposited me in a dark room. It received only a flicker of light from the outside, but this helped me make out what was in it. It resembled the kinds of ghostly rooms you hear about in folktales and legends. I spotted what must have once been a bed but was actually just a metal bed frame. It was covered with a shabby blanket, which I picked up and fashioned into a kind of cushion to place over the skeleton of a bed. My strength was waning, and I desperately needed to rest the weight of my body against something. I felt as if I were in a terrifying nightmare.

## A NIGHT I WILL NEVER FORGET

Terrible silence hung suspended in the air, interrupted only by the sounds of Ramadan prayers coming from the minarets. These were the prayers I'd heard my whole life, but I had never before felt about them the way I did that night. I experienced a strange sense of spirituality that before then I had never experienced. Many thoughts swirled around in my head: I started contemplating what awaited me, what I had to do and say. I had to remain coherent and be extremely cautious about every question and answer. I put my trust in God Almighty. My imagination took me to that place, to Khiam Prison, which I'd had so many terrifying dreams about, about getting locked up inside there. Now this nightmare was coming true. What was it like? What would they do to me there?

Would I ever leave after I'd entered, or would I remain there forever as that cursed man had threatened? Who had given me up? Could it be my friend, as he claimed? No. We'd made a pact and sworn that none of us would talk should we be arrested. But why would he have mentioned her specifically? This was proof that she had confessed to something. But what? What had she said?

I don't know. Many questions zoomed through my mind, but I could find no answers. Suddenly a clear image of my siblings whom I'd left behind at home alone materialized before me. What were they doing right at that moment? What had happened to them?

*Oh, my brother, what did you experience when you saw them? No doubt you thought that they'd come to take you to prison, because you knew nothing about what I was involved in.*

*Oh, my sister, what are you thinking right now? No doubt you're crying, cursing, and swearing. My little sister, what's happened to you? Oh my God, what will happen to you all? Have you even broken your fast, or has fear completely consumed you?*

*I wish I could see you all now or at least hear your voices, but there's no way. What will you do, Mom? I worry about you getting hurt. And you, Dad, what do you think about me getting arrested and taken to prison? I'm your favorite child, what will your great love for me do to you? And my other siblings, what will your reaction be? I'm sure you'll avenge me.*

All of these thoughts plunged me into a state of terror, afraid that my brothers would take some kind of action that would endanger their own lives. I started praying to God Almighty to fill them with patience.

These ideas swirled around relentlessly in my mind all night, keeping me up and completely preoccupied, worried about my parents and siblings. I burst out in sobs, my chest tight with fear and longing to see them, even if just for a brief moment. I couldn't get a wink of sleep that night, except for a few scattered minutes at a time. I felt the weight of this looming sense of evil beginning to crush my soul; the specter of imminent danger hovered over me. I wasn't even thinking about myself—just like anyone else who's been arrested, my only worry was my parents and siblings.

At dawn, I heard the sound of a car pulling up to the center and its motor being turned off.

No doubt they had come to take me to the prison. I called on God to stand with me against these infidels. I looked at the door with trepidation. It opened suddenly, and I pretended to act natural—as if I weren't scared, as if I feared nothing. Fawzi al-Saghir approached me and said,

"Good morning." I did not reply, remaining silent. He continued, "Don't be afraid. I'll do what I can to look into your case and try to get you back home, but for now I have to take you to Khiam."

Despite what he said, I stayed silent. Then he ordered me to go to the car. I left the room, gazing into the distance, offering up my farewell. Then I looked at the car. I thought they might put me in the trunk, handcuffed and blindfolded, since that is how they transported most detainees. However, he ordered me to open the back door and get in, so I did. Then al-Saghir got in the car too, and Kamal Salih joined him.

The time of our departure for that cemetery had come. There were no cars anywhere on the roads. I only saw a few workers trudging down the street to their places of employment, stealing glances at the car with terrorized looks on their faces. It's no wonder of course, because they feared that their turn might come next. I looked around at the trees, houses, streets, and passersby as if it were all a manifestation of beauty and splendor. I stared at a tree and was filled with the strange feeling that it was a sacred thing. I don't know why I was flooded with so many emotions at this particular moment.

Why did everything seem so beautiful, exquisite even, when I regularly saw those same things every day? I'm certain these feelings came from a deep knowledge of my land and its value.

In the meantime, Fawzi al-Saghir put a cassette into the tape player; the first song was about mothers. I will never forget how the opening words rang out, "Forgive me, mother, I am asking for your forgiveness." It moved me so deeply that I burst out in tears the very moment I heard those words. It was as if he was deliberately playing this song to psychologically torture me.

We arrived at a place called Al-Dardara, which had a large pond surrounded by a park. It looked ready to host a concert or a party. The car stopped and al-Saghir turned to face me, "Look at the top of the mountain across from us, that is the Khiam Prison. What do you think? Are you ready to confess yet? We can go back to where we came from, before we've even gone in. But once you enter that place, it's very difficult to leave again. No one who goes in ever forgets it."

I remained silent, my gaze fixed where he was pointing, trying to see this unknown place. It looked like a fortified castle looming in the distance, a man holding a gun standing atop its tower. This collaborator, Fawzi al-Saghir, kept talking, trying to convince me to confess. But I didn't utter one word, as if I couldn't hear what he was saying. What had happened, happened and nothing could change that.

Al-Saghir restarted the car and continued on his way toward the destination. About a quarter of an hour later or perhaps even a little less, the car stopped in front of an iron gate that was about six meters wide. Our journey ended there, and I started examining the place. There were sandbags piled up around the towers and four armed guards stood watch over everyone entering the prison. Al-Saghir, the collaborator, asked one of the armed guards to open up the gate for him so we could enter. But this other agent wouldn't allow the car to enter directly and instead asked Fawzi al-Saghir to show his identity card. Despite seeing it, the guard wasn't sufficiently reassured, and he called another person on his walkie-talkie. I heard him say, "There's a Bint Jbeil security services vehicle here, transporting a girl." It seems that the person on the other side told him to let the car enter, since he stopped talking and motioned to Fawzi al-Saghir to follow him inside the prison complex. The car advanced a few meters and then pulled over to the right where it stopped in a spacious courtyard, surrounded by rows and rows of cells. This was the Khiam prison.

## WHAT IS THE HISTORY OF KHIAM PRISON?

The Khiam prison building dates back to 1933, when French Mandate forces established it overlooking the town of Khiam. In 1943, the Lebanese Forces took the barracks over and made some additional improvements. In March 1978, the Israeli occupation forces seized these barracks. They handed it over to their collaborator and defector from the Lebanese Army, Major Saad Haddad (1934–1984).[7]

In the year 1985, the Northern military command of the Israeli army decided to make this barracks the central detention center for the collaborationist militias under the command of retired Major General Antoine Lahad (1927–2015), who assumed his duties in 1984 after the Israeli collaborating agent Saad Haddad had died. The part of the old barracks they converted was originally meant to be stables for horses.

## THE ORGANIZATION OF KHIAM PRISON

Khiam was divided into sections consisting of a detention center, an interrogation area, and the headquarters of Lahad's militia. These were all built around a main courtyard.

The detention center was divided into five parts, most of which were located within the old French barracks. There were two rows of cells in this section, and each cell door had a peephole covered with a metal grid. Most of the cells had no light source, however some light could filter in through tiny ventilation holes between the ceiling and the walls. A three-meter-high wall topped with barbed wire divided these three areas from the main courtyard. The fourth part of the prison consisted of cells for women prisoners. A fifth building had been added, adjacent to the women's prison. In each section of the prison there was a bathroom, a kitchen, and a guard's room, near the cells.

### Section 1: Prison One, or the Lower Prison

The prisoners called this section "the old prison." But the Lahad militia called it Division 111. This section mostly housed prisoners who were actively being interrogated. It contained at least four solitary confinement cells, each less than one square meter in size. There were also six cells less than two square meters in size, and seven or eight cells that

7    For a brief history of the South Lebanese Army, see our Introduction. MA and MH.

were two meters long and one and a half meters wide. It was sometimes so crowded with prisoners that it earned another name, the Prison Graveyard. Even in the year 1988, they still used extremely small cells in this section, which were only fifty centimeters long, fifty centimeters wide, and seventy centimeters tall, for interrogation purposes. The prisoners called those cells the chicken coop.

## Section 2: Prison Two, or the Central Prison
The Israeli collaborating agents called the Central Prison, Division 122. It consisted of five cells, each of which was two square meters in size and only able to accommodate six occupants, no more. In the year 1986, they added 14 cells of the same size to accommodate the influx of prisoners. This section also had a nurses' station, with a small medical clinic and guards' room. Attached to this second section was a walled-in courtyard for exercise, extending into the main courtyard. It was about twelve square meters large. There was a web of netted barbed wire instead of a ceiling, so the prisoners called it "the Sunroom." They called Cell Five in Prison Two, "The Tomb," because it was extremely dark.

## Section 3: The Upper Prison
The cells in Section Three, the Upper Prison, or what the agents working there called Division 132, were built in the year 1985. There were two rows of ten cells each, all of which were no more than two square meters in size and could hold a maximum of six prisoners each. Section Three had fewer cells of the kind that the prisoners dubbed "the chicken coop." Those were used for punishment rather than interrogation.

## Section 4: The New Prison
At the end of the year 1987, Division 144 was added to the prison. The prisoners called this section Prison Four, or the New Prison. It was built next to the Women's Prison and contained two rows of six small cells, and two additional rows with three cells in each. All of these cells were about three-square meters in size. Cell number 8 was a separate cell of

about four-square meters in size—the largest cell in the entire prison. Prison Four also had tiny solitary confinement cells and a courtyard for exercise.

### Section 5: The Women's Prison
Women prisoners were held separately from the men, in a section near the interrogation area. Section Five was comprised of five regular cells and one solitary confinement cell as well as a bathroom and a room for the female guards. In 1990, they added six more regular cells, another solitary confinement cell, in addition to a bathroom for the guards and an exercise yard.

### Interrogation Rooms:
Though there were a number of rooms used for interrogation in many parts of the prison, prisoners were usually interrogated in five rooms located between Section One and the Women's Prison, next to the Prison Warden's office.

Torture continually took place in these rooms, never stopping—day or night. The screams and moans of torture victims ceaselessly echoed from these rooms all throughout the prison. This is where they flogged prisoners' legs with iron rods, stuck needles into their skin, beat their private parts with whips and metal bars, kicked them with their boots, pulled out their fingernails with electricity, and… and… other methods of torture too numerous to recount…

# GUARDS

Some members of Lahad's militia were lookouts, guarding the main prison gates from posts atop towers on the prison's five corners. These guards had rooms to live in, a telephone room near the main gates of the prison, as well as bathrooms across from the main walls. There were also rooms on the other side of the main gates that they used for meetings.

However, these were transformed into bedrooms for the prison warden and his team of collaborators and agents. Several managers in the prison who answered to Israeli military intelligence held positions with considerable responsibility. The most important of these was Jean Homsi, nicknamed Abu Nabil. He was from the border village of Qlayaa and responsible for interrogations.[8] His deputy, Husayn Faaour, was from the village of Khiam itself and was called Abu Arab. The military commander of the prison was called Amer Fakhoury and he was from the village of Marjayoun.[9]

## ENTRANCE PROCEDURES

The car stopped outside of a room from which a tall, dark-skinned agent emerged, weapon slung over his shoulder. This was at exactly seven o'clock in the morning. I knew what time it was because I'd heard the news broadcast begin in the car.

Fawzi al-Saghir ordered me to get out of the car and go into a room that had doors on either side, leading to more rooms. As soon as I climbed out, the guard carrying the weapon asked me: "So what's up, did you finish Law School?" I stared at him and wondered how he knew I was in Law School. Mere seconds later, I found myself inside a large room where a tall, dark man wearing civilian clothes was waiting for us. I found out later that it was the interrogator named Wael, or at least that's what they called him—they didn't use their real names.

A few seconds later he asked me my name and I gave it to him. He ordered me to take off my jewelry and then went to make a phone call. I could make out only a bit of what he was saying. "Come down

---

8   The village of Qlayaa is located in the Marjayoun district, about 36 kilometers from Bint Jbeil. MA and MH.

9   The town of Marjayoun is located in the district of the same name, about 42 kilometers away from Bint Jbeil. In the year 2019, the collaborator Amer Fakhoury tried to return to Lebanon from the USA where he had fled, but he was arrested by the Lebanese government. The American government pressured the Lebanese for his release. MH and MA.

here and bring handcuffs and a bag with you." Moments later, two young women wearing civilian clothes entered the room. One was a full-figured boxy blonde; the other one, who was rather thin with jet-black hair, was holding iron handcuffs in one hand and something black in the other. She asked me to hold out my hands and I was shocked that she spoke to me in Arabic with a Lebanese accent. At first glance, I'd assumed they were Israelis and would speak Hebrew. She then put a black bag over my head.

I couldn't bear it, so I tore it off. This lady collaborator reprimanded me loudly, "Don't ever do that again." She put it back on and tied a blindfold of the same color over my eyes. I couldn't see anything and felt as if I were suffocating. She tugged the edge of my sleeve and told me to follow her. I asked, "Where to?" She retorted sarcastically, "To the cinema! … Now walk and don't ask questions." Blindfolded, I was afraid of bumping into something, so I followed close behind her.

We walked a few steps and she told me to stop. After this I heard the click of a lock turning, and then the creak of a metal door opening. She ordered me to lift one foot and then the other so I could enter the room. She unlocked my handcuffs and ordered me to remove the bag from my head and untie my blindfold. I did both. I found myself in a room that was barely a meter or two long and half a meter wide. "So this is the place you imagined…" I thought. Then she told me to put my hands behind my back. She locked handcuffs on them and did the same with my feet. She propped me up on the ground and said, "Don't move." Then she left, locking the cell door on me. The top of the metal door had a peephole of scratched up glass which was difficult to see through.

As I took in my surroundings, I felt like someone was putting their hands around my neck. I looked around and thought, "Where am I? What is this?" The first thing I noticed were the words written on the cell walls and scratched into the door. They were the names of young women and men, their dates of incarceration, and also words about their families, their mothers especially, and the homeland. There were also Qur'anic verses. At that moment, I found myself unable to concentrate on any specific thought. I felt dazed, as if I were sleepwalking. Suddenly a very clear image of my family appeared to me—I could see my parents and siblings. My mind was plagued by so many questions about their reaction to my arrest and what would happen to them. Only after this did I find myself thinking about what was in store for me in this place.

I was in Khiam Prison. I'd heard so much about this place. And I'd wanted to go there and share in the experience with those who preceded me in the struggle. But what would happen to me now? Would they assault me, as we'd heard they did to the other girls they'd arrested and detained? Many questions bounced back and forth in my mind, including if they might kill me here. This thought comforted me a little, because what more could they do to me, if I were already dead? I kept ruminating on this for a while, perhaps about an hour and a half, until the sound of the cell door opening interrupted me, and I jumped up, startled.

The woman agents had come back, put the bag over my head, and blindfolded me again. After this, one of them undid the shackles binding my feet and ordered me to follow her. She held my hands loosely, ordering me to take one step down and then another. I realized that the cell they were putting me in had two steps down. Then I walked about thirty steps straight ahead until she ordered me to lift my foot up and then lower it. After that she took the bag off my head. My hands were still in handcuffs. I found myself in a room that had a metal cupboard, three beds, a table, and a chair. A young man not more than 25 years old was sitting on the chair behind the table. I looked right through him and saw a number of files. He opened one and started questioning me. "What's your name? Where are you from? How old are you? What do you do? Where are you studying? How much do you weigh? How tall are you? Do you have distinguishing marks on your body? Did you have any surgeries before coming to prison? Do you suffer from any illnesses?" I answered all these questions, and he recorded the answers in the file in front of him. When he finished, he asked the female guard to get me a mattress and four blankets.

She came back and put the bag and blindfold over my head and led me to a place that was only a few steps from where we were. I entered the room in which I was supposed to deposit my mattress and blankets.

Then she unlocked my handcuffs and ordered me to pick up the mattress and two of the blankets—not all four—and follow her out. Upon exiting the room, I noticed a pile of mattresses—maybe fifteen, and blankets strewn around on the ground. I reassured myself that these mattresses were surely for the other prisoners who must be behind these walls, but I couldn't hear a sound. Everything was quiet except for the sound of the wind. She accompanied me back to the cell, retying my hands behind my back. Then she left and locked the door.

I put the mattress on the floor. It was made of spongey material, no more than three or four centimeters thick, and was wrapped in thin plastic which made a squeaky noise that put your nerves on edge. As for the two blankets, their stench almost made me lose my breath. I sat on the mattress and propped my head up against the wall. I got lost in my thoughts again. I felt like I was in a nightmare. I didn't know what was happening around me. I felt my eyes grow heavy from everything swirling around in my head. I don't know how long I was suspended in this state between sleep and waking. Then the squeak of the cell door made me start in terror.

The door opened and there was a new face in front of me. She was not the young woman who had brought me to the cell, and it wasn't her colleague either. Perhaps there were more than just those two. I examined her. She was in her forties or a bit older. She was plump, short-statured, and had piercing blue eyes. She asked me my name and where I was from, then ordered me to stand up. She put the bag over my head, saying, "I advise you to confess to everything, it's better for you to do that than to be tortured. I'm trying to help you." I responded, "I don't know anything. So I can't confess." She then answered back, "You all say the same thing at the beginning and it later turns out that you actually do have a lot to confess to." After this, she told me to lift my feet and then lower them again. I realized that there was a high edge or step that I had to climb up, several paces away from the cell. Then I took several more steps forward and she led me somewhere and asked me to sit on a chair. She held it out with one hand while holding onto me with the other.

I hadn't detected the presence of anyone else in the room, but suddenly I heard static and choppy sounds of Hebrew coming through. I realized it was all coming from a radio transmitter. I tried to focus intently on my surroundings, trying to hear everything going on, and I gathered that there was someone else in the room. That's when I became aware of the sound of notepad pages rustling. I focused my attention more seriously on the source of the sound, then I was surprised by a voice asking me, "What's your name?"

He had started my interrogation. The fateful day was Friday, April 21, 1988. I jumped at the sound of his voice. He had taken on a harsh tone. I answered his question and he carried on, "Where are you now, Nawal?"

"As far as I know I am in the Khiam Prison."

"How do you know that?"

"Because when I was taken to the center in Bint Jbeil they told me that's where they were going to take me."

"What do you know about Khiam Prison?"

"I don't know anything about it."

"Nothing at all? Aren't there other people from your village here?"

"Yes."

"So, what have you heard about them?"

"All I've heard is that they were tortured."

"So, you do know that someone who is brought to Khiam is tortured. But do you know why they are tortured?"

"No."

"And why are you here?"

"I don't know that either."

I wanted to believe that the person speaking to me was the very same Fawzi al-Saghir who had brought me to the prison. The similarity was in the harshness of his voice. I tried to lift the bag from my head to verify this and I called him by name, that is to say, Fawzi al-Saghir. I glimpsed his face for a few seconds only. As a result, he started shouting at me,

"Pull that bag back down and don't you ever do that again!"

The quick glimpse I had caught of the man revealed that it actually wasn't Fawzi al-Saghir but someone else. I had made out very little of him, but I did see that he was heavy-set, bald, and about fifty years of age. He said, "You told me your name is Nawal, right?"

"Yes."

"Look, Nawal. I'm going to be honest with you, and I'm going to help you as much as I can. You're an unmarried girl here and your situation is rather delicate. I'm sure you've heard of many other people we've brought here. Engineers, teachers, doctors, religious clerics… They all confessed to everything after having originally denied it. We've made even the hardest men cry. No matter how long you continue to deny knowing anything, you'll eventually confess, because we have many ways to extract your confession."

He started enumerating all the barbaric torture methods that they used, including electric shocks, lashings with whips, alternately pouring hot and cold water over you, kneeling for hours on end. He listed all these many methods and more that I cannot even recount because of how cruel they were. He described all of these savage methods of torture, then asked me, "What will you do? You're a young woman. Don't expose yourself to any more insults and torture, honor is important to an unmarried young woman. You understand exactly what I'm saying, don't you? If it comes to it, and you were to be assaulted, it would be your own fault. But if you want to preserve your honor and dignity, and not be subjected to insults, to be treated decently, you must be honest and confess to everything in detail. You shouldn't deny anything, and most importantly you should recount everything. In detail."

I listened to this introduction closely, as I did his threats against my honor as a woman, and I replied, "I've already told you that I don't know anything. You don't believe me, but I know nothing, not even why I'm here." This conversation lasted about half an hour. Then there was silence. When he started again, he went back to asking me about my name. He took handwritten notes of my answers to his questions. He repeated all the questions he'd asked about my age, my profession, my life, where I completed my studies, the number of people in my family, their names, ages, workplaces, places of residence—every big or little thing about my life from the day I entered the world until that very moment we were sitting there.

I could tell that he was writing all of my answers down, from the way his papers rustled. I didn't know how much time had passed, but I started feeling suffocated. Even though it was cold outside, I felt my body temperature rising. Hours passed with me in this state. After I'd finished answering all of his questions, he stopped for a bit and then again offered his advice and guidance. He told me, "Go back to your room and think things over very well. Think about everything, even things you might consider trivial. Afterwards we'll bring you back for another interrogation. I advise you to confess because if you deny your involvement, you're going to see so many things… and then you're going to understand how lenient I've been with you." I heard him ask the guard to come and take me back to the cell.

While we were heading back, she told me, "My advice is: confess everything. You'll be better off." I was taken back to the cell and thanked God over and over again that this session was over, as it was getting more and more difficult to breathe. Inside the cell, I found a loaf of bread on a red plastic plate, and a dish of fava beans. My thoughts ran away from me, and I asked myself, "How can one human being possibly treat another like this?" I'd heard that they treated prisoners like animals, and the extent of their hatred and contempt for us pained me. I couldn't shake off the feeling that I was on the verge of suffocating, about to pass out. I sat down on the mattress, leaned my back against the wall, and found myself thinking about the interrogation from another angle. Why all of the specific questions about me and my family?

Was this what they wanted to know about? I don't think so. What is the point of all of these private questions? An image of my family appeared vividly before me, and before I could realize what was happening and without my control I burst into tears, sobbing hard. I felt that

I needed a long, deep sleep—my head hurt a lot. It only took me a few minutes to drift off, even though I could hear all kinds of noises outside. There was the sound of a car, then footsteps, then people talking. I don't know how long I was in this stupor, but I remember panicking when I suddenly heard my cell door being opened. I thought that they were taking me to be interrogated again.

The guard opened the door and ordered me to grab the plate I had found in my cell and take it to the bathroom. She pointed it out to me; it was right across the hallway about ten steps away from the cell. She looked at the plate, which was exactly as it had been when I found it. She shouted at me, "Why haven't you eaten your food yet?"

"I'm not hungry."

"You have to eat, or we will force you to in another way."

"When I'm hungry I'll eat. Now I only want to drink."

"Don't you have a pitcher of water?"

"No."

Then she asked me if I had a small bucket in the cell, and I told her I didn't have anything at all. She asked me to bring a bucket from inside the bathroom and put it inside the cell with me. I asked her, "Why do I need this?"

She replied sharply, "This will be your toilet inside the cell. We're not going to open the door for you every time you want to use the bathroom. You'll use the bucket inside the cell except when you leave at mealtime."

And how awful this "bathroom" was! It was nothing but a plastic bowl made out of a large shampoo bottle. Then she took me back to my cell and left.

Later, I heard all kinds of sounds coming from outside again, unusual noises, and the shuffling of feet. I tried very hard to make out what was going on. I started feeling around for any kind of hole or opening in the cell door through which I would be able to peer out. With effort, I could see under the cell door. But all I could spot there were girls' feet—a group going up, and then a little later, another group. No doubt they are the women prisoners. Where are K. and F.? Where are the two of them now, what had happened to them?

The sounds from outside kept me occupied for some time, but after a while I no longer saw anyone. It seemed that these women had finished their work. I sat back down on the mattress. I was assailed by my thoughts again. I don't know how long I remained frozen like this before dinner came. This time it was one boiled egg, one boiled potato, and two pieces of toast. While she was delivering it, the guard asked me to go to the bathroom and wash out the bucket. But I didn't have to because it was still empty. She locked the door and left. Not long afterward, I once again heard footsteps outside my cell, and I tried to concentrate on what was happening around me. I hoped to catch a glimpse of K. or F., but I didn't. And then, once more, everything went back to how it had been.

Whenever it was dark outside, the cell was flooded with darkness too. There was no light at all, except the very little that reflected off of the glass peephole on the door. I lay the mattress out on the floor and put one of the two blankets under my head, after wrapping it around itself in the shape of a pillow. I tried to sleep while anticipating what might happen to me. I would doze off but wake up whenever I heard a sound outside. A couple of hours passed, and suddenly I heard the sound of metal scratching against the ground near my cell door, which made me jump out of bed. Afterwards, I heard my cell door opening. There were two guards. The lights outside were somewhat bright. One of them approached me, saying, "Get up!" She picked up the handcuffs off the floor—that was the metallic sound that had frightened me—and locked them around my wrists. She put the bag and blindfold over my head and eyes as usual and led me away to the unknown.

At last we stopped walking, and the guard led me into a room that I felt was further away than the room I had been taken to the time before. There were also more obstacles blocking the path on this walk than on my previous walk. She put me in the room, sat me on a chair, and then left. It was so silent that I was fully convinced that there was no one else in there but me. But I suddenly realized I was wrong and was disappointed by the sound of rustling papers. I knew for certain that there was indeed someone else in the room. I remained seated, still, and there was no noise at all except the sound of pages turning. It was clear that I was now all alone except for this person I was seated across from, but I didn't know who it was or what they looked like.

A voice broke the silence, making the following statement: "Yes, Nawal. As you now know, K. and F. are here. And you also know that they have confessed everything." He mentioned some of what they had confessed about me. "They're going to leave here soon. If you want to leave and go home, you'll have to confess everything like the two of them did. If not, you're going to face a world of pain." I didn't respond, and he carried on, "We know everything about you. K. and F. confessed everything about you to us. So that you never have to be faced with any insult or injury, it's best if you simply confess every detail—however big or small. You have two choices. Either you confess to everything, or …" He paused for a moment and then continued, "You're a young, unmarried woman. This lands you in a delicate situation. Don't expose yourself to anything you will regret. A young woman who doesn't confess might face an assault. We might put her in the middle of the prison courtyard naked, and then bring all the male prisoners out to look at her, and most of these men have been inside the prison for a long time, if you know what I mean."

His words sliced through my body and soul. I pondered my bad luck and sinister fate. Would they really do this? Had F. or K. really confessed? And so quickly? I could hardly believe it. His calm manner of speaking cut like a surgeon's knife. His threats were so severe that my blood froze in my veins. But somehow I had a strange feeling that what he was saying wasn't true and that he wouldn't do this, although you couldn't put anything past these traitors. After he laid all this out on the table, he then reminded me once again that my comrade had confessed. If I wanted to be free myself, I had to do the same as she had. This interrogator then ordered me to be returned to my cell and asked me to think about everything I had been through. I went back to sleep—or, rather, to that state of non-sleeping. Hellish thoughts returned to play in my mind. I was in this state for quite some time and then found myself starting in terror when I heard the door being opened once again. The guard was asking me to pick up my mattress and my things and follow her. I asked her, "Where are we going?"

"Don't ask questions. Pick up your things and follow me."

I did as she asked and walked behind her for a distance of about twenty meters from where the cell was. Then she put me in a room that was somewhat larger, the size of a normal room. After I'd gone in, she stated, "This room is bigger." Then she left, locking the door behind her. I started examining this new place. The room had an aluminum sink, a faucet, and a wooden door leading to a second room, which I ventured into. This one was very tiny, the size of the previous cell or a little bigger, with concrete pillar about a meter high. At the upper edge of the pillar was a window to the outside. My curiosity led me to climb up there to see what there was outside. I could see barbed wire surrounding the whole place, and through the wire I could make out a number of villages that I didn't know at the time. I later came to learn they were the villages of Marjayoun, Qlayaa, and Kherbeh.[10]

I looked around and could see a guard atop a tall tower, standing behind sandbags, holding a rifle. I was afraid he would see me because he was looking right at me, so I got back down on the floor. I examined the room itself once more, especially the walls. Then I spotted something very strange—a sort of funnel made of aluminum, hanging down from the ceiling a little bit, such that it stuck to the wall near the main door. It was about a half the size of a barrel. I kept looking at it and a terrifying thought suddenly occurred to me—perhaps this was some kind of instrument of torture. No doubt they use it to hang prisoners and torture them, or perhaps there is some sort of surveillance device in it used to listen or take pictures inside the room. Many such thoughts occurred to me as I tried, in vain, to figure out what it was for. Then I moved on to try and make out what was written on the walls of the room. Mostly they were names of

10   Kherbeh is a village in the Marjayoun district, about 35 km from Bint Jbeil. MA and MH.

prisoners. They'd scratched them in the wall along with the dates of their imprisonment. The vast majority of these dates were between the years of 1986 and 1988. So many of them... I stopped at each for a moment before passing onto the next one, imagining the person who went with the name. Where are they now? Have they been released?[11] Or are they still here? I went over to the faucet and unconsciously turned it on. I put my hands under the water and washed my face several times before gulping it down like someone who hadn't tasted a drop of water for a long time. Then I moved over to my mattress and sat down, returning to my thoughts, but unable to focus on any specific thing.

I finally felt somewhat sleepy and closed my eyes, surrendering to a deep slumber. After an undetermined amount of time passed, I woke up to the sound of the muezzin's voice, which I could hear coming from outside the prison, from the town of Khiam. The sound was clear and true, as if nearby. I focused on the recitation of the Qur'an. Then I heard the cell door opening. The guard entered and, unusually, was smiling at me. "This room is larger than a normal cell," she said.

I told her that it didn't matter how big the room was if you're locked inside. She replied, "Get ready! The interrogator is coming here, and you have to tell him everything in detail. This interrogator is more lenient than the other one and will treat you well. But it all depends on you. I'm just trying to help you out." Then she stopped speaking to me and announced loudly, "Come in Mr. Awwad." This was the code name of the interrogator she'd just introduced. I learned later that his real name was Issam Jarwani and that he was from Deir Mimas.[12] He was about forty years old. He came in and greeted me with a sly smile, full of deceit. I realized then that he hadn't just arrived at my cell and walked inside—he'd been there the whole time, standing outside the door to eavesdrop on my conversation with the guard.

He asked my name, my age, and my profession. I answered. He then

---

11    About three thousand people in total were held in Khiam Prison, nearly four hundred of whom were women and children under twelve years of age. MA and MH.

12    The village of Deir Mimas is located in the district of Marjayoun, about 35 kilometers away from Bint Jbeil. MA and MH.

handed me some blank paper and a pen saying, "These papers will help you think. You have to write down everything that happened with you and your two friends, in detail. Don't leave anything out, however trivial or insignificant it may seem. If you want to speak to the interrogator for any reason related to this investigation, all you have to do is knock on the guard's door and tell her, 'I need to speak to the interrogator.' Think it over carefully. You have until midnight." It was about seven o'clock. He pointed to the lamp hanging from the ceiling, saying, "I'll leave the light on in your room until morning so you can write." Then he left with the same smile on his face—one filled with guile and unspoken threats. The guard followed him out, locking the door behind them.

I put the papers next to the sink, and started talking to myself: "What does he want me to write? Why does he want me to write my confessions in my own handwriting? What should I confess to?" I wondered if he'd asked my friends to do this too and if they had written everything down. What a disaster it would be if they'd actually done that! Where are they now? Perhaps I could speak with them… I felt a raging headache, as if my thoughts were frozen in my brain. After thinking it over for a long time, I decided not to write anything down, but then I hesitated again. After going back and forth with myself, it occurred to me that I could write down the information they'd already confronted me with. The information that F.Y. had given them. I started writing that down, and I filled up about two pages. I reread what I'd written several times and felt my headache getting worse. It wasn't the normal kind of pain; it felt like the impact of the thoughts colliding in my mind. I went to bed to lie down a little and decided not to write any more. I wouldn't say a thing, no matter what happened. What could they do to me? Is there anything worse than death? I didn't care if they threatened or tortured me. I made this decision quickly, to get it over with. Every minute felt like an hour. It is so difficult to feel every minute pass. The time had come. I knew it because I heard the sound of the door opening, and the interrogator speaking to the guard. They walked in together.

He asked, "Did you finish writing? I hope that you have written everything down. Show me the papers." He started examining them and said, "Is this all the information you have? In any case, I warned you from the beginning. You'll see what's in store for you here." He repeated this over and over, "Is this all you have?" "I wrote down everything I know," I said. He snarled in response, "What are you saying?" I repeated my answer, more loudly this time, and that I didn't have anything more to add.

The interrogator left after asking the guard to lock the door. He left me alone to think. Many thoughts raced through my mind. Did he really know I was hiding things? What will he confront me with next? What did F.Y. confess to? Why does he always fixate on her and not K.Z., though they were arrested together for the same thing? I couldn't tell. I fell into a deep sleep, like someone finally resting after completing an arduous task. I felt nothing after that. Only fear of waking up in a panic, because I knew the door would open again, which was just a prelude to the handcuffs and the bag over my head.

This is of course what happened. The guard came and spoke to me sharply, "Come on, get up now." I remained motionless for a moment since I felt I was dreaming up the whole thing. She kept barking. I got up and faced her. She was standing near the door and asked me to hold out my hands so she could cuff them. She then put the bag over my head and blindfolded me. She led me down the usual path to the interrogation room. She asked me to sit down on a chair she was holding out for me. I couldn't hear anything around me, and I imagined that there was no one else there. But then a voice surprised me, "So Nawal, how are you? What's it going to be? Inshallah you've thought things over well?"

I didn't answer the question. He kept talking, "The information you've mentioned isn't new to us. These are things we already know, just like we know the whole truth about you. You're better off confessing everything of your own accord. Your confession will lighten the punishment you'll receive. Only after you have finished with this full confession—and we'll be the ones to determine what a full confession is—will we release you. But if you continue denying that you have more information to disclose, your punishment will be more severe. Perhaps you'll even die and be buried here. You only have two choices."

I answered him with words that sparked his anger. "I wrote down everything I know. I don't know anything else. I wrote the whole truth."

"You're a whore and a liar. If you carry on with your denial and lies, we'll have to try a new style of interrogation. You haven't seen anything yet. But it seems that this softer touch isn't working on you." He moved on and asked me directly about the specific accusation that I'd denied: my knowledge of the weapon and silencer, and more specifically where I'd procured them.

For the first time, I denied the source I'd gotten it from. But after an intense argument, during which he'd used all kinds of obscene language, he mentioned the name of the girl I'd gotten the weapon from, but without her family name. I realized then that one of my friends had confessed this because they were the only two people who knew about it. This girl had close ties to the resistance and was related to a fighter who'd supervised my weapons training. She was the source of the weapon; she lived permanently outside of the occupied zone and was the one who'd delivered it to me. I told him sharply, "Then what she said isn't true—I don't know that girl and I'm prepared to face anyone who informed on me and said this."

He laughed sarcastically and responded, "You're the one who's lying, do you think that you're fooling us? Do you really believe that interviewing prisoners is that simple?" He then went back to his aggressive tone, "Denying this won't help you. This is your final chance. Who is this girl, and where does she live now?"

"I told you, I don't know anything about her," but before I could even finish my sentence, he punched me hard and shouted, "You'll confess eventually, no matter how hard you try to resist."

He started savagely beating me on my face with both fists. His blows were powerful and made me lose my balance. I fell on the floor and he pulled me up by my clothes saying, "Get up. This is nothing!" When he said, "I'll be back to torture you, but in a different way next time... Then you'll write down everything that I say you should," I thought he was going to leave. But I don't know if he actually left the room or not. A short while later he asked me again, "So will you confess now?"

"Should I confess to something I didn't do?"

He exploded, "Confess where you put the weapons and the other equipment!" I told him I didn't have any weapons or equipment. He yelled at me again and beat me brutally. "You're a liar, you damned woman." Then he pulled me by the arm and threw me to the ground, stomping on my shoulders. He started kicking me with his shoes on. I kept repeating, "I don't know anything." This only made him more enraged and he tortured me further. He started lashing me with a whip. He forced me to touch it with my hand before he whipped me with it. Then he started to prepare the electrical wires by braiding them together and slapped me with them all over my body and head. It was incredibly painful. All the while, he cursed and swore at me, his words mingling with whatever I managed to choke out. Whenever he made an accusation, I repeated my denial.

Suddenly he pulled me by my handcuffs and stood me up. He walked toward me and ordered me to stand near the wall. He lifted my hands above my head such that they were suspended in the air, not touching the wall. He said, "You must stand like this all night. You may not lower your arms."

It was very cold outside, and the sound of the wind whistled in my ears. After a little while, it could not have been more than a few minutes, I heard footsteps. I looked down from under the bag to the ground. Perhaps I might be able to see something, I thought, but I couldn't. Suddenly I felt ice-cold water pouring down over me. I gasped from the surprise of the water and from sheer terror. The water was accompanied by the interrogator's voice. "Tonight you will experience all kinds of torture, but you can save yourself by just confessing."

He had not been the one who poured the water over me. His voice was too far away. What more will they do to me? There was nothing more they could do, except kill me. This brought me a lot of comfort.

If I confessed to something, they would only accuse me of more things, because they would know that I'd been hiding things from them. So I decided not to confess anything at all.

My surroundings went silent. I could hear only the howl of the wind and distant footsteps. I remained like this for a long time. My strength gave way, and I started shivering so hard my body shook and my teeth chattered like someone with a high fever. I felt I was on the verge of total collapse. I didn't know what time it was; I had been in this state for what seemed like hours. But suddenly I heard the guard's voice ordering me to put my arms down. She grabbed my arms telling me to follow her. I asked her, "Where are you taking me now?"

"It's not your concern, you'd have been better off if you'd confessed. So, let's go. No more questions." A little while later she ordered me to stop and then undid my handcuffs, saying, "Take the bag off your head." I did and looked around. She had brought me back to my cell—thank God. When she tried to leave, I asked, "How can you leave me like this? It's so cold and my clothes are all wet."

"I'm not bothered, actually. I don't care. And frankly, it's none of my concern. You're the one who did this to yourself. Now you have to deal with it," she said to me cruelly. "You're all the same. In the beginning, you say you don't know anything then afterwards it becomes clear that you're all killers." She locked the door behind her and left.

I was frozen in place for a moment. I looked around to take in my situation. My body was shaking. I needed to come up with a plan to dry out my clothes, but how? It occurred to me that I could take off my outer layer of clothes and hang them next to the window. Perhaps they would dry by morning, which would arrive soon. Meanwhile I could wrap myself in a blanket. I did that and sat on my bed with my hands wrapped around my legs. They were quaking from the cold. Suddenly my situation really dawned on me and I wondered if the guard would come back and take me to the interrogation room when I was in this state of undress. But I told myself that she'd just have to wait until I put my clothes back on. I sat like this, thinking about so many things, wrapped up in a blanket that afforded me some warmth, until I fell asleep. But I was barely asleep for more than a moment because I was so nauseous and the cold compounded everything. Dawn soon broke. After the sun's rays started filtering in, I felt my heart calm slightly because the warmth might ease my suffering, if only a little. The cold had penetrated deep into my marrow. I tried to get up, but my entire body was throbbing in intense pain, which I had not felt so strongly since right after I'd returned from the interrogation room. My fingers hurt immensely, and my back would not support me standing up. I needed desperately to go to the bathroom. What to do? I couldn't use the bucket, my makeshift toilet in the cell.

It occurred to me that I could knock on the door, especially since I could hear sounds outside—footsteps, the sounds of cars. I did this but no one responded until a while later. Then I heard the guard's voice asking me what I needed. I told her. She said to wait until it was my turn to go to the bathroom. We were only let out at specific times to use the bathroom, each cell had its own designated time, and this was done in order.

Finally, my turn came. The guard was not the same one who'd been there during the interrogation. I later found out that she was nicknamed Souad, but her real name was Sonia and she was from one of the villages in the Marjayoun district. She brought me a cup of water and a plate to put my breakfast on. It consisted of a cup of tea and a piece of cheese. Then I was supposed to go to the bathroom and fetch some water to clean the cell. After I'd finished, she asked me what my name was and when they'd brought me here. Then she locked the door on me once again. After about two hours, this same guard came back carrying a bag and handcuffs. I knew that this meant an interrogation and that she was taking me to the room where it would happen. She led me there, and once inside, I realized that the room had a heater because I could feel its warmth. She told me to sit down on a chair.

I did so silently, paying close attention to what I could hear around me. It seemed that I was in a new interrogation room, one I hadn't been taken to before. Suddenly I heard a voice calmly say, "Take the bag off your head, Nawal." It was a new voice. It felt strange but I did as I was asked. Then I looked around and found myself at a desk. Sitting on the other side was a man of about forty years of age, tall and thin with gray hair. Later I learned that he was the warden responsible for the prison and was called Abu Nabil. His real name was Jean Homsi, and he was from the village of Qlayaa. It seemed that this room I was in was his office, because it had a desk, a cabinet, a diesel fuel heater, and simple furniture. It was quite organized.

This prison warden started speaking to me in a calm voice. He explained that their goal was not to oppress the prisoners. They just wanted to know the truth... whatever it was. Whether a prisoner had done something big or small, they would regain their freedom. Whatever I'd done was my right, because I was defending my land and my dignity. I was very surprised that he said this, but I quickly figured out that it was his way of luring me into disclosing information. The way he was speaking, it was as if we were just having a chat. He started talking politics, and I immediately understood that he was trying to determine my party affiliation. He told me, calmly and without missing a beat, that I would be better off if I confessed everything while I was in Khiam because if I didn't, they would move me inside Israel itself.

I feigned stupidity in the kinds of answers I gave to his many and varied questions. I told him that I hadn't done anything important other than what I'd already confessed to. I could tell that he was convinced that I was hiding a great deal and that I'd done more than the trivial things he was already aware of. The way he looked at me and spoke to me then changed and took on a more cruel and intense tone. He asked me if I had been tortured, though the signs of torture clearly showed on my hands and face. He said that this was nothing. He then once again laid two options before me, just as the others had done: confess or experience more severe torture, be transferred inside Israel, and perhaps even be assaulted. He followed up by saying, "We're going to give you a chance to think it over. You should know that whatever you're trying to deny, it won't do you any good." He went on and on, telling me that young men who'd seemed as strong and steadfast as mountains collapsed and confessed in the end, and then were released. He only used the expression "released" to encourage me to confess, because the people he mentioned—Ali Saghir and Rafiq Dabaja, both from Bint Jbeil—were imprisoned for more than ten years.

This conversation went on for about an hour and a half. When it was finished, he told me to put the bag back over my head, but without the blindfold this time. Moments later, the guard took me back to my cell after she had chained my hands together again. But she returned me to the tiny first cell I had been in, not the larger one I was being kept in most recently. She made me move all my things from one to the other. I wondered why I was being taken back to the cell where you can't breathe, where you feel like a giant boulder is crushing your chest and you want to scream at the top of your lungs. This is psychological, nerve-wracking torture, and yet another form of their torment.

The day ended without them calling me back to be interrogated, though I was expecting it at any moment. Night passed and nothing happened. This was another color on their torture spectrum: they'd make the prisoner live in a state of constant anticipation. I wondered what had happened. Were they convinced that I didn't have anything more to say than I already had? I didn't know.

The next day passed the same way, without anything happening. But in the evening, the cell door opened, and the bag and handcuffs followed. The guard led me to the interrogation room. Based on the distance that we walked to get there, it seemed like the same room I'd been tortured in the first time. There was a new interrogator whose voice I hadn't heard before. He started talking to me, asking me my name, what I did for work, and some personal information. Then he moved on to the subject of the interrogation and asked me if I was still insisting on denying everything. I said that I was not denying anything—I simply had nothing to say other than what I had already told them.

The interrogator showed an interest in what I had to say, and I thought that he would treat me decently, because he was speaking quite calmly at first. But my hopes were quickly dashed when I sensed that he was approaching me, and more so when I glimpsed his feet from under the bag on my head, which only allowed me to see directly below me. Suddenly he grabbed me by my shoulders, hard, and said, "You'll confess no matter how long it takes. We can stay here all day. You're better off if you just confess." I repeated what I'd told him, but he confronted me with some new information pertaining to the operation that I had been involved in. He said that I had been keeping tabs on one of the collaborating agents who lived in a house close to ours from the roof of our house. I denied it, but he insisted that one of my friends had supplied this information. Though what he was accusing me of was true, I continued to deny it.

He carried on, "You should know that we have all the information about this. And there's lots of it." I kept repeating that I didn't have anything to confess to, and that only increased his wrath. I knew he was going to do something to me. But what? He took me by surprise and attached the electric wires to my hands. He began torturing me—even though my fingers were still raw from the first set of electric shocks I'd received. I felt like my heart might stop beating. My screams grew louder and louder as the electric shocks came more quickly and intensely.

He stopped so he could resume his accusations, of which there were many. Some were true and others I knew nothing about, like me having a detonation device, which wasn't true at all. He focused on how I could have received weapons training. He moved on from electric shocks to whipping. He came up with elaborate ways to torture me until I collapsed and was no longer able to speak. This is really a brief snapshot of the torture methods used in this prison. Minus the continuous beatings, repeated orders to confess, and obscene language and cursing, the interrogator couldn't charge me with any specific, explicit accusation. The only thing he cared about was extracting a confession from me, any confession, that he could present to his boss, thus proving his competence. It didn't matter if the confession wasn't true. They took me back to my cell after almost two hours of continuous torture. I no longer had the strength to stand or even sit. I was just laid out on my mattress in a moaning and groaning lump. I started pleading with God to stand by me, to deliver me from the merciless hands of evil. How could they know mercy, when they had sold out their country, their conscience, their religion, and their very identity? *I entrust everything to You, Almighty God.*

This distress call relieved me somewhat, but at the same time, it triggered me and made me cry. But I couldn't determine precisely why I was crying. Was it the pain? Was it the situation I found myself in? Or was it because I was so far from my family? As I mentally went over what had been done to me during that interrogation, I looked at my hands that had started to turn dark blue where the blood had pooled. I can still recall the colors of torture that this miscreant used against me. I almost couldn't believe that something like this could happen on earth or that an ordinary person like me could endure such terrible torture. I surrendered to exhaustion, but I really didn't sleep much at all...

My eyes were closed, but my entire body was throbbing in pain. A bit after midnight, the sounds of screaming coming from the torture chambers interrupted my slumber. This kind of activity never stopped in Khiam—day or night. The screams and groans of torture victims constantly echoed throughout the prison walls.

This was a young man's voice. I was taken over by an intense fear. Then the terrifying thought occurred to me—and I don't know why I imagined this—that the person screaming in terror was my brother. I forgot about my own aches and pains and sharpened my senses to discern whether or not it was my brother's voice. Though I figured out that it was definitely not him, I continued to fear for the fate of that young man and kept listening to know when his torture session was finished.

This is the sense of sisterhood and brotherhood—with all the meanings these words carry—that prisoners feel for one another. They love each other with the sincerity usually reserved for sisters or brothers who are daughters or sons of their actual parents. I called upon God to stand with this young man. *Oh God, please be with him and keep these oppressors away from him.* They were torturing him, no doubt using electric shocks. The sound of this young man's screaming—or that of any young man—is even more painful to hear than that of a young woman. Who is he, I wondered? The cell they had put me in was close to the interrogation chamber. The sound of his screaming was audible and clear, and I could even make out some of what the interrogator was saying as he roared, raining curses down on the tortured prisoner.

From time to time, the young man would once again call out, with bloodcurdling shrieks. He would beg and plead, in that way that makes you feel helpless despair, as that damned interrogator rained down obscenities and curses upon him. When I heard this young man shrieking like this, however, I forgot my own pain and felt imbued with some sense of power because I felt that I was sharing in his torture and suffering. He was not alone.

These strange thoughts restored some of my determination. Things continued this way for a few days: I experienced different flavors of torture meted out against other people while I was in the cell. The sounds of moaning infiltrated my cell every day, almost constantly. The interrogation room the sounds were coming from was one where they used electricity and whips for torture. Administering electric shocks was a method they used on nearly every prisoner. No one was spared. They would put wires on your fingers, ears, chest, or some other place on the body and shock you. Similarly, they flogged you with an instrument that was like a magic wand: it transformed from an ordinary stick into iron chains, a whip made of fiberglass, or braided electrical wires. Everywhere on your body would sting afterwards.

If none of those worked, the torture would take on a different cast. It can be like a farce, like what unfurled when I, or any other prisoner for that matter, was arrested. You might spend long hours in front of one of the interrogation rooms across from the prison's main square. I was surprised there once by a bucket of cold water, which was dumped over my head, followed rapidly by another bucket—this time of hot water. After that, you are moved to a cell, all wet, without any dry clothes to change into.

You're tortured and the director of this farce—the interrogator—claims to know everything; he'll convince you of this, just to trick you. They keep you separate from everyone else, making the others invisible to you. It's like the Blind Bear game, which everyone loved in child-hood—you'd reach your floppy hands out in front of you, blindfolded, trying to find the other children playing the game. But this is not the same. This is a death game, arms bound in handcuffs, and legs weighed down by iron or plastic shackles. The master of this game controls everything. And you have a bag over your head, which prevents you from even seeing the hateful bastard's face. You're in a terrible position: you fall asleep one moment and wake up another. Even in the chill of winter, hot sweat pours down from your temples so profusely it washes your face and clouds your eyes. And you know they do this because their eyes don't dare meet yours. Then this bastard comes back, telling you that he knows everything about you. He'll throw you in a cell with wet clothes, you'll feel the ground against your skin, no part of which has been spared the lashes of the whip, which you continue to feel over and over again in your memory. The place is known and unknown at the same time: an unknown location, but a known fate. The interrogator returns and claims once again that he knows everything about you. But if this is true, why is he so afraid of you seeing his face? He'll blindfold you and bind your hands while he punches or kicks you with his military boots.

He claims that he knows everything. His lexicon is overflowing with heavy-handedness, cynicism, indecency, insults, obscenities, and curses. Reality looks dark, gloomy, and depressing, filled with nothing but humiliation and death. The hateful interrogator is mainly concerned with humiliating you and hearing you burst into tears, as you beg him to loosen your shackles or take the bag off your head because you're suffocating. He's broken a stick over your head, perhaps cracked a rib or damaged an internal organ, maybe a tooth or molar has flown out of your mouth.

As quickly as your tongue pronounces the words, "I don't know anything," the torturer raises his whip to lash you like a brutal beast, wrestling you with all his strength, in a rage-filled dance. This is where your ears take center stage, taking over for the other senses, because they are better able to keep up with everything unfolding around you.

Another bastard comes in. From under the bag, you feel him holding the shackles that press against your wrists. He drags you roughly, throwing you to the ground to beat you. You fall and find yourself face to face with a lifeless corpse lying on its face or back, or you bang against something else in this room, which is outfitted with all the latest innovations in torture devices.

All of this went on and on. I'd been in the prison several days when I was surprised to once again hear the voice of Abdel-Nabi Al-Jalbout. I could distinguish it from the others and recognized it even from inside my cell. He was talking to a new prisoner. "We wish you a happy stay, G." Upon hearing these words, I immediately lay right down on the ground and tried to make out any tiny detail from under the cell door. No doubt this was G.A., a young woman I knew. The interrogator had asked me about her during one of my interrogation sessions. I didn't know of any operation she'd carried out and I didn't think that she was even active. Why would they have arrested her? On what grounds?

The piece of information I was missing was that F. Y. had entrusted her with a task. But I only found out about this in prison, after my arrest and hers. She'd been in charge of writing down the names of the civilian guards who were forced to be on night duty in Bint Jbeil. Their names were broadcast over the mosque's loudspeaker in town. The Israelis and their collaborators imposed this on all the young men in town. G.A. didn't know why F.Y. had asked her to do this. She was arrested and detained for a year and a half because of it, during which she endured the bitter hardships of prison and all the torture that comes along with it.

## INSIDE INFORMANTS

After my first interrogation and torture session, I was left in the cell for several days without being called back. I thought that they'd been convinced by what I had said, and that my interrogations were over—or almost over, at least. But I didn't know that they would follow up with another style of extracting my confession. They moved me to a new cell, which had the number two hanging on the door. There were two other female prisoners inside who welcomed me. I looked at them like they were creatures from another planet. I felt relaxed at first because being with other prisoners might bring me some relief. Being transferred also added to my deluded belief that I would be released soon. What I did not know was that they were about to lead me into a new kind of interrogation. A traumatic incident happened when I was with these two prisoners which led me to discover that they were actually collaborators and informants.

This happened in the very first hour I spent with L.B., who was from the village of Rab al-Thalathine, and Z.M., who was from the village of Qantara.[13] The one called L.B. started asking me why I was in prison and telling me the story of her arrest. She cursed and swore about the interrogators and the harsh methods they used against us. She said that anything we did to resist these enemies was our right, and that we should've actually done much more.

I didn't know that she was saying all that just to trick me into confiding my whole story in her. All along she was only trying to get me to tell her about the kinds of activism I'd been involved with, whom I was working with in the resistance, and all kinds of other things. She spoke openly and freely about what had happened to her and didn't hold back any details. She very well might have been inventing imaginary operations that she hadn't really carried out. Still, I didn't say much and was cautious about confiding in her.

---

13   Rab al-Thalathine and Qantara are villages in the Marjayoun district, 25 and 20 kms from Bint Jbeil, respectively. MA and MH.

This was a completely different approach for gathering information. After having been in prison for some time and having experienced the torture of interrogation, the sincerity and frankness of these informers comes as a relief. But this is all part of their game. The sincerity is just another trick intended to deceive you and lure you into confessing to the informer—whom you are mistakenly led to believe is a friend. This sincerity is only meant to make you feel bad for being cautious and speaking very little and lying—in other words, concealing the truth. But after the interrogation is done, and after you figure out that this so-called friend is indeed an inside informer, the entire situation is reversed: you become the one in control. You become sincere and frank, the one who doesn't care about a thing. And in this turn of events she becomes the liar—and a real liar, not the type she made you feel like you were. She becomes cautious about her every movement both inside and outside the cell, because of the ongoing collaboration between her and the guards.

There were no limits to the lengths she would go to curry favor with them. She had the right to leave the cell several times a day, outside the schedule that had been set for us, which only allowed us to leave two—or at most three—times a day. A pack of cigarettes and a lighter caught my attention; I asked her if they were allowed. The other woman in the cell, Z.M., said that it wasn't allowed, but that you could have them in specific cases with a doctor's note. I later learned that this privilege, the cigarettes and lighter, was one of the temptations the Israelis used in dealing with their collaborating agents. Z.M. didn't leave the cell as much as L.B., but I later figured out that she was no less a collaborator than her friend. I gathered as much from their partially audible secret conversations. Whenever we talked all together, it inevitably turned to the issue of my arrest and the reasons why I was in prison.

The two of them kept bringing this up, to the point that L.B. started trying to convince me that I should confess whatever I was hiding. She claimed it would ease the burden I was carrying. She kept trying to push me to confess, saying it would make things easier, especially since my interrogation was not over yet: she explained that my case wasn't actually closed, which meant the interrogations could resume at any moment. Only closing my case would mean the end of interrogations and torture, she told me. The two of them had done that—they confessed everything, and they were waiting to be released in a few days. Though I didn't yet know that they were informants, I was still very cautious speaking to them; I didn't reveal any information that I'd concealed in the interrogation. I only shared the things I'd already confessed to. The informer L.B. kept trying to get me to confess—she kept insisting, and on the third day that I was with them, while we were talking about confessions, she asked me once again to confess and ease my conscience. She even went so far as to suggest that I knock on the cell door and ask the guard to take me to the interrogator. I could then tell him that I'd remembered new things I wanted to confess to. She even started knocking on the door herself, but I stopped her, repeating that I didn't have anything to add other than an unimportant, really minor incident that I'd told her about. I insisted that this incident didn't matter and really wasn't a big deal—it was just about a collaborator who lived near us and spent most of his time on the balcony of his house with another collaborator.

At that moment, the guard opened the door and asked us to come out, so we could use the bathroom and take showers. We left our cell. This was the first time I'd been told to shower with other women. It surprised me that we had to wash together in front of each other. I felt reluctant, and L.B. exploded laughing, "If you carry on like this you'll go without a shower unless you get put into solitary confinement. I'll have to inform the guard about this." And she did.

The guard then came and began reproaching and reprimanding me—these are the rules and they cannot be disobeyed, she said. I came up with the idea of only washing my hair. But what would I do later on? Would I remain without a shower? I found out soon enough. When the time for the next shower came, I was forced to shower in front of these two informers, even though I'm so shy I can't even change my clothes in front of my own mother and sisters.

It's as if they had come up with this system to shame and humiliate you. But they don't know that they are the ones stripped down—of any humanity, dignity, and honor. Despite their hateful system, we remain clothed in our dignity. Even if we feel embarrassed and humiliated, they are the ones who are despised by all. After washing up and putting on the clothes I'd been given by the guard, that had previously belonged to other women prisoners, we went back to our cell.

We sat in front of the cell to try to catch a bit of the sun and dry our hair. But this barely lasted ten minutes because the guard showed up and told us to go back into the cell. She kept L.B. outside, however, on the pretext of her cleaning the guards' room, something that is done by prisoners who are no longer subject to interrogation. They also clean the interrogators' rooms, as well as the actual interrogation rooms themselves, as experience later taught me. That afternoon, the guard opened the door at a time outside the schedule and called my name. My heart quickened when I saw the bag and the handcuffs. I wondered what was going on. Would I be led back to interrogation again? There were still visible signs of torture on my hands and body.

The guard took me to the interrogation room next to the men's prison—Prison One. The interrogator started off using his "soft touch." He showed me the information that I'd written down, and what they'd accused me of. He followed up saying, "All of this information means nothing to us. We're convinced that you're hiding a lot more." I started repeating that I wasn't hiding anything, but he screamed in my face. He mentioned the name of the collaborator—Abu Saffah—who lived near our house. I was surprised and realized that L.B. was the one who'd given him this piece of information. The interrogator kept cursing and snarling in my face. Then he brought out new forms of torture to use on me. He started off with a whip that ate into my flesh. I experienced intense pain at the beginning but then my body went numb and I no longer felt the bite of the lashes as I had the first ones.

After a while, he stopped to give me a final warning, as usual. All of the interrogators did this at the end of questioning. He threatened that if

I didn't confess everything now, my fate would be disastrous. He hinted that I would be assaulted, but he was giving me one last chance.

When he was finished, the female guard came back and put me in the bathroom where she ordered me to kneel down near the sink. She started pouring cold water and then hot water over me. She stopped to warn me not to stand up or even move a muscle. I remained like this for about an hour. Then I sensed footsteps and the voices of a number of different prisoners. They were talking to the guards about filling up water bottles and emptying the buckets that they were using as toilets inside their rooms. But the guard told them to be quiet and not talk so much.

The bag still on my head, I tried hard to feel around for something or speak to someone. But I couldn't because the guard stuck to my side like a shadow. A second guard was taking the prisoners to the bathroom, according to the schedule. Then a voice called out to me by name, telling me not to be afraid. It was the voice of a woman prisoner, but I couldn't tell who she was. It could have been K. or G. or any other prisoner. This raised my spirits somewhat.

The prisoners finished the work they were doing, and silence reigned once again. I felt an intense exhaustion and fatigue wash over me all of a sudden. It was as if the voices I was listening to had distracted me from the situation I was in. My body was shivering from having to wear damp clothes in the extreme cold. Whenever I felt any hint of movement near me, I thought it would be the guard coming back to take me to the cell. But this didn't happen for another two hours, maybe even more. When she did take me back, Z.M. greeted me with a horrified look at the state I was in. The informer L.B. had painted a smile on her face for the guard, who had asked them—both informants—to convince me to confess. Then she left.

I just stood there for a while, completely silent, staring at them like someone looking at their enemy. But Z.M. broke through my silence and gave me some of her clothes to wear instead of my wet ones. I took them because I desperately needed to change out of my damp clothes. Then I sat on my mattress and kept quiet, staring at the door whenever I heard any movement outside. L.B. started asking me about what had happened to me. I didn't answer at first because I was convinced that she was the reason I was in this state. If I had been able to, I would have wrung my hands around her neck and strangled her right then and there. What had happened to me made me all the more convinced that I shouldn't utter even one bit of information about my interrogation to them. I was sure that she was reporting every conversation we were having to the interrogator.

I eventually broke my silence and started telling her what had happened to me in a tired, weak voice, to show her that I had no more information to disclose. Despite this they didn't believe me. It was as if they wanted me to invent any kind of story to confess to them. Feigning ignorance and acting as if she had no connection to the matter, L.B. said, "We just can't win. Even if we confess everything, they still tell us that we're hiding something." She was trying to show me that she had nothing to do with what was happening to me now. Then I replied, "It's so strange that they're paying so much attention to trivial matters. Everything that happened to me now is the result of a stupid, unimportant conversation about a collaborator, who just happens to live near my house. Can you imagine?" I followed up, "No doubt F.Y. informed them about that. Because I'd told her about that person." My point in saying this to the informant was that she would definitely pass on this conversation to the interrogator and she would tell him that I had no further information to hide. In any case, that's what I was hoping she would pass on.

The morning following this incident, work went on as usual. We had to clean our cells, go to the bathroom, fill up water, wash out all our containers, which had originally been boxes for sweets, and then take our measly breakfasts, which were barely enough to sustain us. Then our cell doors were locked. I was still in pain from what had happened the day before, and silence wrapped itself around me once again. I did not speak except in generalities or about things with no connection to the interrogation. Seven days passed like this after the incident. The guard returned after lunch on the seventh day I'd spent in the cell with the two informants.

After she'd finished distributing all of the lunches to the prisoners, she opened the door to our cell and told me to pick up my mattress and all my things and follow her. "Where are we going?" I asked her. She answered, "Walk in front of me and no questions." After we left the cell, I stopped and wondered if she had the bag and handcuffs with her. But I saw nothing and just followed her to cell number seven. This is the suffocating cell I had previously been in.

"Why did you bring me here?" I asked. She replied, "Don't ask questions." She locked the door on me and left. Oh God, why did they bring me back to this cell which makes my suffering so much worse? I stayed there for two days without any interrogation. On the third day, the guard returned and ordered me once again to pick up my belongings. This time, I didn't ask her where we were going. The important thing was that I get out of that coffin. She led me to a room between Cell Seven and Cell Two. It was Cell Four.

She opened the door, put me inside, and then left. I looked around. There were two other prisoners there with me. I don't know why, but I felt calmer just looking at one of them. She was called Z.A. and was from the town of Qantara. Her goodness showed on her—"their mark shows on their faces," as the Qur'an says about the faithful (Q 48: 29).

The second woman was called J.S. She was from the town of Kfarhamam.[14] For some reason, I felt cautious around her, though I didn't know anything about either of them yet. Z.A. welcomed me with a pure and sincere smile, and then helped me arrange my mattress. From there we started introducing ourselves to each other: our names, our towns. Then I asked her how long she'd been in prison. She answered me with the same smile that never left her face, "Six months." I was surprised by that and asked her why. She smiled once again but audibly this time, "For nothing."

---

14    Kfarhamam is a town located in the Hasbaya region, about 57 kilometers from Bint Jbeil. MA and MH.

I asked J.S. the same question and she said, "A month and a half." But Z.A. interrupted her elaborating that she was in prison with her sister and cousin. I was even more shocked and asked her anxiously, "Where's your sister now?" Later I learned that her sister's name was N.S. and her cousin was called R.K. They were both informants for the prison interrogators.

She told me the numbers of the cells they had been put in and I asked her, "Do you ever see them?" She said that this was forbidden, each of them was in their own cell. Z.A. interrupted her to tell me that K.Z. had been with them at one point. I asked her eagerly, "Really? Where is she now? How did she seem? How's she doing?" With her ever-present smile she assured me that she was well, her health was good, but she was consumed with worry about me.

"Worry about me? Why?" I replied. She said, "We could hear your screams while you were being tortured, and K.Z. was really upset." I asked her, "Did she tell you anything about why we were arrested? Did she have any information about G.A. or F.Y.?" She told me what K.Z. had said about her interrogation. She told me that she had been tortured a lot, and despite this didn't confess to anything, but that F.Y. had confessed to everything—she hadn't held back even one piece of information. And that was why they had acted out all their anger on K.Z. and me. F.Y. had also been tortured, and this is why she had confessed to everything so quickly.

I suddenly remembered something that had been bothering me and asked her, "Do they really assault girls here?" She smiled as usual and told me calmly, "Don't worry, that's just a threat they use to compel young women to confess, but they don't ever do it. They might tear off a girl's clothes and leave her naked, but that's just to put on a show and intimidate us." I interrupted her, "Has this ever happened to you?" She sighed and replied, "Yes. I hope God never forgives them and takes revenge on them." I asked her, "Who tried to do this to you?" She mentioned the name of the interrogator and his nickname "Awwad," the one from Deir Mimas.

She started to tell me about their different interrogation styles. I cut her off again, "He's the one who tortured me so much! He stepped on my fingers." I showed her where his blows and those of others still showed on my body. She had also been tortured with electric shocks and was lashed with a whip. As she described the torture she'd been subjected to, I understood very well that she had also been through hell, but she was here in front of me now, doing fine. "When did your interrogations stop?" I don't know why I didn't dare ask her about the reason she was in prison. Perhaps it was because I had become wary of talking about this.

She carried on telling me that the interrogations had lasted for about a month before they closed her casefile. I asked her, "How did you know that your file was closed? Did they stop torturing you then?"

She answered, "Yes, but if they find out something new, they'll call you back in for interrogation and start torturing you again."

"Has this happened to you?"

"No. But I have no ties here to any other male or female prisoners. Your situation is different."

"How do you mean?"

"If one of your comrades confesses to anything new after they close your case, they'll open it up and call you in again."

Out of the blue, I asked her about G.A. She answered me with a nod of her head, "She's OK. About the same as you. May God forgive F.Y. She didn't hold back any information about any of you." She followed up by telling me that F.Y. had implicated me in her confession and I asked her breathlessly, "How?"

She replied: "When they brought her here, they put her in the room with the sink." I told her they'd put me in that room as well. She continued, "Under the sink on the ground, there is a metal disk with holes in it that let the water drain out. In lieu of prayer beads, she used the circular holes to complete her prayers.[15] When she finished, she

---

15    This is the Istikhara Prayer that people turn to when they are hesitant about something and need guidance. They recite verses from the Holy Qur'an while using prayer beads to consult God. If you finish your prayers and there is one bead left in the strand, this is a good omen. This is what F.Y. did using the drain holes. NB.

knocked on the guard's door and asked her to call the interrogator in. She confessed everything about you then." This piece of information made me really angry with F.Y. Was that supposed to make any sense? Is she crazy? Z.A. told me that K.Z. was really angry when she heard as well, because when they'd gotten arrested, she'd urged F.Y. not to give up any information about me. But F.Y. gave in with the first slap and simply confessed everything. Time passed quickly. This young woman did reassure me somewhat, despite the anger rising inside me over what I'd just heard from her. The second woman in the room, J.S., had been listening to the whole conversation that transpired between us, and interjected from time to time, sharing what it was like when she was interrogated.

I felt an urge to lay my head on Z.A.'s chest. I needed a deep sleep. I was like a baby in need of a mother's embrace. Though this woman was only about two years older than me, the way she spoke, her face, and her features made her seem motherly somehow. Or maybe it was just that I really needed a mother and a family to get me through this situation.

The three of us started arranging our mattresses so we could sleep. We then exchanged a few more snippets of conversation. She asked me what the situation was like on the outside. New prisoners are the only conduits of information for what is happening out in the world. We were in a new world in prison, cut off from everything else.

Every morning was the same routine: cleaning our rooms, going to the bathroom, and having that excuse of a breakfast that wasn't even enough for a child. Then every other day, a shower, unlike the male prisoners who could sometimes go for a full month without washing. I stayed in this cell for a few days, during which I became more familiar with a lot of things, including the guards' rotating work schedules. There were three teams of two, and each team worked for two days and then was replaced by another.

We had many varied conversations in that cell, but most of them revolved around our families. I learned from Z.A. that she had lost her mother when she was young, and that she was the only girl in a family of male siblings. Her father was elderly, and her new father's wife came to visit her every month and a half. When she mentioned family visits, I was suddenly crippled by an overwhelming sense of anxiety. I didn't understand why. But then I pictured my mother coming to visit me, and I understood. How would I look her in the eye? How would I be able to face her tears? Far from bringing me comfort, these thoughts only made me extremely anxious. I started fervently hoping that no one in my family would visit me because that would simply reinvigorate this tragedy, both for me and my family. The days passed and it was soon to be Eid al-Fitr. I thought that they would maybe release me soon, since I had now spent about a month in prison. But then the door opened again, the bag and handcuffs right there with it.

At about ten in the morning one day, our cell door was opened off schedule. The guard called out my name and told me to put the bag over my head. She shackled my wrists. My heart was beating wildly; I wondered what new could have happened. She led me to the interrogation room where a new interrogator was waiting—just as I had begun to think that my release was imminent.

The interrogator asked me about a young woman and man who lived in my town, Bint Jbeil. I suspected they'd been arrested. Why else would the interrogator be asking me about them? I knew very well that whenever a name was mentioned during an interrogation, arrests would ensue. He intensified his line of questioning about the girl, M.A. I denied any knowledge of her, except that she was from my town. He then asked me to remember what he was about to say: "I will ask you what your name is. Only then can you answer." What I didn't know was that this would very soon confirm to me that this young woman had indeed been arrested.

It was silent for some time, then the interrogator asked me once more, "What's your name?" I responded, as instructed. But I was stunned to hear M.A.'s voice, answering the same question about her own name at the same time. I couldn't tell who the question had been directed to.

The interrogator wanted me to give false information about M.A. But when he asked me about her, I said that I didn't know her or anything about her. "Shut up," he snarled. He started swearing and cursing then ordered me to be returned to my cell. I was surprised that he didn't torture me, given the situation.

I was returned to my cell and found my two friends anxiously waiting for me to be brought back. They wanted to know why I was being interrogated again after all that time. I told them what had happened. I was becoming increasingly worried about M.A.'s fate here in prison, but my friend Z.A. calmed me down and soothed my fears. She reassured me that this young woman wouldn't be stuck here long if nothing could be proven against her.

That night, M.A. started screaming at the top of her lungs. If I had been worried before, I became much more so now. It sounded as if she was being tortured with electric shocks. I was completely paralyzed by fear: partly because I was terrified of being called back in to be tortured once again, and partly because M.A. was undergoing torture herself. I sat up on the bed, anticipating what would happen and listening attentively to what was going on outside.

I couldn't sleep at all that night I was so preoccupied with what M.A. was going through. The following morning, news of M.A. being there had spread through the windows of all the cells. We learned that F.Y. had named her in her confession—she'd mentioned her under interrogation. F.Y.'s cellmate passed this news onto us. She took advantage of F.Y.'s absence from the cell to tell us everything. F.Y. had indeed started collaborating with them, which meant she could leave her cell very often. Her cellmate also told us that F.Y. had mentioned the name of a blind girl, who had then been arrested and held for a day before being released.

This information was like a stab in the back—why did she do this? Was it the torture? So many other prisoners had been subjected to the most horrific types of torture, but they didn't confess so easily. Even if they did, they didn't just give up all the information they had. But F.Y., it seems, had confessed to everything on her own, without the extreme pressure other prisoners had faced and endured.

I went back to living in a state of fear and anxiety. I didn't know what would happen next. Everything was compounded when K.Z. was moved to a new cell. I tried to find out why from the rest of the prisoners. It turned out that F.Y. had informed on her and disclosed new information that she hadn't shared at the beginning. Then we received another piece of painful news, something we hadn't expected would happen. K.'s brother had been caught and wounded during an operation that he was carrying out with his resistance comrades. The prison administration informed K.Z. of this in an effort to torture her further, psychologically this time.

Questions started to be raised about F.Y. Was she collaborating? How else could she have known this information? All the women prisoners were asking the same questions about her, and they all eventually learned that F.Y. had definitely become a secret collaborator.

That's so cheap... Was it that simple for her to just abandon her principles, conscience, and faith? And for what? For freedom? What kind of freedom do you have if it's in return for what she did?

Two days after this incident, right at the time we heard the sunset call to prayer coming from the village mosque in Khiam, my two friends and I were eating our dinner. Our cell door was opened, and my heart jumped once again. Surely I was being taken for interrogation. The guard led me out of the cell as usual. On that night I experienced all manner of physical and psychological torture. I will never be able to forget what they did to me. The interrogator took a harsh approach from the very beginning of that interrogation. He tried to trick me into thinking that he wasn't Lebanese but Israeli (and in a way, it was true: he and those like him, all those who betrayed their country, never truly belonged to our nation and people). He spoke to me using masculine pronouns and broken Arabic. He indicated he would use all kinds of torture, and then came the usual threat that he would have me transferred inside Israel soon because I was keeping important information from them. His voice was like thunder. I repeated over and over again that I had no new information and wasn't hiding anything. He interrupted me, addressing me as a man, saying, "Listen, I will have no mercy on you."

I would try to interrupt him, but he rejected all my attempts—still addressing me in masculine pronouns. "When I say you will confess, that means you will confess," he kept repeating. I wished that I could have seen this interrogator's face, the same way I had caught a glimpse of his shoes—he was wearing civilian shoes. Then he left suddenly. When he returned, he tried to trick me into thinking that he was not the same person who had been questioning me just before. This time, he took on a Lebanese identity. (How could a scumbag like him claim to be Lebanese?) He claimed he wasn't Israeli. But I was sure it was the same man. He had the exact same voice. He started advising me to confess to him, rather than to the other (imaginary) person. But no matter who was asking, my answer was one and the same.

Then he raised his voice. "Where did you put the detonator?" he asked. I was surprised by his question and answered that I knew nothing about a detonator or about anything else. He said that F.Y. had talked about this in her confession and that he was confronting me with facts. He then moved onto another line of questioning, "Who tasked you with assassinating Abdel-Nabi?"

This was a disaster. I answered, "No one put me up to it. I came up with it all on my own." He poured all of his wrath down upon me; he started beating me with the whip and kicking me with his feet. Then he stopped and laughed sarcastically, "You must be very important. You're the one who plans all the operations, right?" I didn't say a word.

He quickly followed up, "But your sister says differently." That sentence knocked the wind right out of me. "We brought your sister in and she's under interrogation as we speak. She confessed everything about you." I felt as if I might pass out. I was extremely shocked. I asked him anxiously, "Why? My sister has nothing to do with anything, and she knows absolutely nothing about what I do."

"She says that you tell her everything you do."

"That's not true, no one in my family knows a thing about any of this."

This made me forget my situation and the pain I was in. My sole preoccupation was now my sister. I couldn't stand the thought of anyone in my family experiencing the torture and torment I was facing. Suddenly

I heard a young woman's scream and almost fainted. I thought that it was my sister. So he wasn't lying! I listened to the voices very attentively, trying to distinguish if I could hear hers. The interrogator then started confronting me with new and different accusations. But I couldn't focus on a word he was saying. My only concern was my sister. I couldn't make out the sound of her voice. On he went with his psychological torture. He said, "Not only did we bring your sister here, but we also destroyed your family's house. The rest of your siblings have been expelled from town. You destroyed your family. I'm telling you that concealing any information from us won't help you. You'll spend the rest of your life here." The screams of that young woman were still ringing in my ears as he barked at me once again, "Confess! Where did you put the detonator and the weapons?"

I needed to know what had happened to my sister, so I answered, "If you want to know, just write down everything you're saying. I'm willing to sign it and take responsibility for every allegation you make. But I'm telling you for certain that my sister knows nothing. She has no connection to this whatsoever."

"We don't invent charges and attribute them to prisoners," he sneered. "They're the ones who have to confess to them." He confronted me with new information once more. I was prepared to endure my torture, and he willingly obliged.

This damned investigator was taunting me with the information he was hurling at me. He was certain that his intelligence contained truths and falsehoods, and he kept trying to get me to confess. He resumed his psychological torture, using my sister to break me.

I no longer felt time or anything else. I only regained consciousness when he stopped torturing me and stopped those horrific tactics he'd been using to scare and terrorize me. It was too much for any human mind to endure. Psychological torture is far worse than physical torture.

He finally ordered me to be returned to my cell, assuring me that he would certainly be back to continue his interrogation another time. I went into the cell. Once the door was locked, my friends immediately asked me what had happened. But before they could even finish their questions, I had thrown myself on the bed and dissolved in tears, sobbing uncontrollably.

My cellmates kept insisting that I tell them what had happened. They sat beside me and tried to calm me down. Weeping, I answered, "They brought my sister N. here. I don't think I can bear it." One of them asked, "Where is she?" I replied, still in tears, "She is under interrogation, I heard the voice of a young woman being tortured with electricity."

"Are you sure it's your sister?"

"I couldn't be sure about the voice, but the interrogator said it was my sister who was being tortured. What do I do now? How can I find out if it's true?" I was getting hysterical. Z.A. tried to calm me down, and J.S. was also trying to assuage my fears. "Put yourself in my shoes," she said. "My sister is here too, but what can we do about it? Maybe your sister really is here, but maybe she isn't.... just try to remember that we'll manage to get some answers soon and find out what's really going on." Z.A. tried to distract me and steer my thoughts in a different direction. She started asking about the torture methods he'd used against me. "What did he beat you with? What did he say to you? May God take revenge on him."

But my own torture didn't matter to me anymore. I no longer cared what they accused me of. The only thing that mattered was my sister. My cellmates kept repeating the same thing: "Let's wait until tomorrow and find out if this is true. Inshallah this is just another one of their ploys, putting you under extreme psychological duress so that they extract the confession they want from you. They're using every trick under the sun. They go around claiming they've brought in our brother, father, sister, or mother—any family member—to manipulate us and get us to confess. But eventually we find out that none of it was ever true." These words calmed me down a little. But the thought that my sister could actually really be here kept gnawing at me. It was making me hysterical. The night passed, though I don't know how.

I'd spent the entire night waiting impatiently for morning to come. At long last, our cell door opened for the scheduled cleaning time. I left the cell like a bird whose cage door had been flung open so it could fly to freedom. This aroused the attention of the guards because I wasn't even pretending to do any work when I stepped outside the cell. I didn't even bother carrying any cleaning supplies. The guard stopped me and asked me what was wrong with me and where I was running off to. Why wasn't I helping my cellmates with the cleaning? I didn't respond to her questions. Put another way, I wasn't even listening or paying attention to her. I needed to get to the bathroom. Perhaps that's where I could find some clue that would confirm or disprove the news. I knew for example that whenever a new prisoner was brought in, she'd be taken to the bathroom to shower. She'd leave the clothes she'd been arrested in in the bathroom and would change into the prison uniform the guards had given her. The new prisoner would not always be allowed to lay out her own clothes herself—instead, this task would most often be given to the old prisoners, so that the incoming prisoner would not become too familiar with the prison layout too quickly.

Once inside the bathroom, I looked everywhere. It had a long corridor divided into several little stalls, all of which could be accessed through one main door. I didn't find anything. I felt a strange sense of reassurance tinged with anxiety.

The guard called out, "Hurry up, girls, let's go." I went back into the cell, and my two girlfriends caught up with me. After we finished cleaning our cell, the door was locked on us once again. "Tell me what to do? What should I do?" I asked them over and over. My nerves couldn't take it. Trying to figure out how to calm me down, Z.A. proposed another way to check if the news were true—something other than inspecting the clothes in the shower. I asked her breathlessly what it was. She told me that when breakfast came, we could figure it out. I asked her how, what did breakfast have to do with it? She replied that she knew how many prisoners there were, and she also knew the different types of breakfasts that usually rotated. She would base her analysis on this information. "When they give us boiled eggs for breakfast, which I think they will today, we always get one egg each. So if the number of eggs equals the usual number of prisoners, that means there is no one new."

A few moments later, the guards arrived to clean cell number two. After having been in prison for a while, prisoners grew to learn what every movement outside their cells meant. They could even tell which cell door was opening at any given moment. We heard a guard's voice calling out that the kilfa had arrived. The kilfa, in this case, were the male prisoners entrusted with delivering the food to the rest of the prisoners. In other cases, they could also be doing heavy cleaning, pruning the trees, refurbishing some of the areas in the prison compound, or preparing the food in the prison kitchen—all under the supervision of the guards.

My cellmate Z.A. said that we would find out for sure, now that the kilfa was here. We started listening keenly to what was happening outside. We practically held our breath. I lay down on the ground behind the door, holding onto the edge tightly. Perhaps this would make the sounds of what was happening outside clearer. They finished cleaning Cell Two, and we heard the guard saying to the people inside, "Take your breakfast," and then close the door. They moved onto Cell One after this. After cleaning it, they said, "Take your breakfast."

"How long will this take!?" Z.A. exclaimed. We could hear them opening Cell Seven, but the sounds of their footsteps were approaching. "Pay close attention," my friend told me, "Didn't I tell you?" My heart was pounding with the opening of the cell door. I asked my friend, "Which cell is that?" It was the door of Cell Three closing. Then the footsteps began approaching our door, Cell Four. I jumped up from my spot on the floor and stood behind the door. "Take your breakfast girls." The breakfast was boiled eggs, olives, and tea. My cellmates took them, and I pretended to help but I was quickly trying to count how many eggs were left so I could know the overall number they were serving. After they finished, the guards went to Cells Five and Six. After this, we didn't hear the sound of any more doors opening. That's when we did our calculations to figure out the number of eggs. In the end, the number of eggs was equal to the number of prisoners, which my cellmate had already calculated to be eighteen. About a quarter of an hour later, the guards came back and opened the door to Cell Two. I asked my friend, "Why are they opening up that cell again?"

"Maybe they are starting to clean the interrogation rooms? After they clean the prisoners' rooms, they do the interrogation rooms, and then the prison offices. They call this the kilfa of the female prisoners."

My two cellmates reassured me that my sister wasn't here. This calmed me down a lot, but I was still worried. After this incident, the days passed slowly and nothing new happened. Eid al-Fitr was coming. It was a glimmer of hope on the horizon. Many prisoners pinned a lot of hope on this occasion. Perhaps they would release a number of us on the holiday. It didn't matter whom, it was just important that people be released. The day before the Eid, just before sunset when only a few strands of sunshine were peeking through the clouds, we looked out the cell window and chatted about our families. I wondered how we would spend the actual holiday. No doubt it would feel sad. My neighbor in Bint Jbeil, the mother of a prisoner, always started off her Eid crying and wailing about her son, praying to God on behalf of all mothers to be reunited with their children.

It was a very moving moment, sitting in the prison like that. It made you miss home, and it pushed you to imagine all types of things. How do prisoners bear the holiday in here? Yet here I am now, enduring what others can only imagine, this painful, heart-wrenching reality. You can't help but cry. And then the faces of your family members come to you, one by one. You embrace them all together as one in your heart, so eager to hold them close.

The morning of the Eid arrived. Time passed miserably. The sun didn't shine. Nothing happened. A sad silence enveloped the place, each and every cell. Tears and silence, which then turned into screams—heads and fists banging against the walls. These damned walls and these damned distances. The holiday passed and nothing happened.

Everything went back to normal. Routine work, boredom, restlessness, and complaining. But we didn't know that there was someone who would deliver us a belated Eid gift and make this holiday different than any other, giving it an entirely new meaning. We suddenly heard the sounds of a powerful explosion, and we all jumped up to look out the windows. Smoke was rising from near the Marjayoun barracks, and we all chanted together, Allahu Akbar.

The very same people whose voices had grown raspy and tired from screaming were the ones who started chanting and shouting. The explosion was the result of an operation led by men in the resistance. I was imbued with a strange feeling that restored meaning to my life in prison. We all understood this resistance operation to mean, Happy Holidays to all of you! Liberation is coming... It was led by the heroic fighter Abdullah Atawi who was martyred—I can't recall what year exactly. Singing broke out in all our cells and rose out through the windows. We sang "Ghabet Shams El Haqq." How many times had we sung those lyrics before? But this time it was different, this time they embodied our reality: "We refuse to die!"[16] From another cell, words to different songs challenged our reality of pain and suffering: "Khiam prison, the beating heart of the South..." Then our voices sang out, "I call upon you and hold your hands tight."[17]

But the moment in which you reach the apex of these optimistic feelings of defiance, endurance, and freedom, you're silenced by the sound of intense beating on the cell doors. It was the female guards. We got down from the ledge we were standing on inside our cell. It was a concrete ledge about half a meter high, of the same width as the cell. We used to keep our things on that elevated surface. And if we climbed up, we could see outside. In just a moment we were all back to our usual places in the cell, joy radiating off all our faces. We sat and asked each other questions: Do you think there are wounded? Did they get anyone? They must have... then, someone said, "That terrible sound alone is enough to shake these traitors to their core."

Time passed unusually quickly that day. When night started to fall, our lights were turned off earlier than usual. On a normal day, they'd be

---

16  Lyrics to a Julia Boutros song, "Ghabet Shams El Haqq." MA and MH.
17  Lyrics to a song by Ahmad Qaabour, "I Call on You." MA and MH.

turned out at around 9:30 PM by the female guards, who controlled this from their station. Perhaps this early plunge into darkness was punishment for our behavior, their revenge against us.

But it didn't matter. In such a place, light and dark are alien concepts. You don't always use your sense of sight. Your hearing is center stage.

Conversations carried on quietly inside the cells and through windows. One person conveys her expectations to another, while someone else passes hers on to her neighbor. Tomorrow will bring new things, no doubt. We all fell asleep with hope for this coming day that would bring us news we needed desperately to hear. Morning came, and it began with the sound of the doors opening, announcing our usual work routine. Our turn came at six in the morning. We were looking at the female prison guards with eyes full of defiance and aggression: How had they spent the previous night?

Exhaustion—or perhaps it was fear—showed on their faces. Really the captors had turned into the captives, the guards into the prisoners. They fear every one of us. We're defenseless and behind bars, but we are free, and they are captives. Our morning work finished, and we sat down to eat breakfast. We all had the same wish for each other: that it would be our last breakfast inside the prison.

We were all focusing on what was happening outside, trying to make meaning out of it; we observed every step the guards or anyone else took.

I asked my cellmate, "It seems like there's some unusual movement outside, do you think there might be a release of prisoners after what happened?"

She replied, "If there's a scheduled release, it will go forward, but it won't happen before 9 AM. In such cases the warden shows up in person to call on the guards. If he does, that'll mean that something is definitely happening."

We went back to surveilling what was going on outside our cells. I never would've thought that the sense of hearing could stand in for the sense of sight like that. It was the only sense that helped you discern what was unfolding around you. You visualized every movement you heard, and eventually you'd become capable of distinguishing the footsteps of a prisoner from those of a guard or an interrogator, or even from the footfall of Zionist soldiers. They would come on the pretext of conducting inspections of prison conditions, but in reality, they were there to check the course and results of various interrogations, and to suggest new methods of torture that would force prisoners to confess.

A strange thing about these visits by Zionist officers is that every time they came, there was a cleaning campaign just before their arrival. The prison guards dictated the cleaning protocol to the prisoners. It began inside the cells and rooms, including interrogation rooms and the main courtyard. When they visited, the Zionist officers would stand at the door of a cell after a guard had opened it and ordered us to turn our faces toward the wall. The Israelis would then start counting us. Why? Were they afraid of desertions? Sometimes the Israeli would look us straight in the face, and just like that, the face of the female guard would melt away. Dissolved into his shadow, she'd go on and on, informing him of our every move. She'd assure him that there were no problems here. It was almost as if she was expecting a reward. How despicable they all were!

Some of these Israeli officers would sometime talk to us in Arabic, asking questions like, "How long have you been here?" And the prisoner would answer with a smile harboring a thousand meanings and her own question, "When will you release us?"

"Soon, very soon."

He and his entourage would then leave and lock the door behind them. The full procedure didn't always transpire in every cell. They usually only looked inside one or two. Actually, this was most often the case. And then we'd sit around wondering what the actual purpose of these visits could be, what information they could be obtaining by asking us how long we'd been detained.

Eid al-Fitr passed, and then several more days after that, and no one was released. We all started to feel disappointed and restless. There was so much grief in the air—maybe if it could explode, the force of the blast would break open our chains. But still we pinned our hopes on the dawn of each new day.

By then, I had spent about a month and a half in prison. It was June 3, 1988, and there I was, being dragged back to the interrogation room once again. I wondered what had happened. Did they have some new information they were going to confront me with?

The bag went back on my head, the handcuffs around my wrists, and once again I was plopped up before the interrogator. I'd thought I was done with all this, with this bag on the head that made it impossible to see anything but the thinnest shred of light slipping through the tiniest of holes. Why the bag and handcuffs, anyway? I'd become familiar with the methods and styles of interrogation, and I even knew all the different interrogators and their pseudonyms. This time it was Wael, the one who received me when I first entered the prison. I recognized his voice. He started out by asking me my name. But why? He knew it already! No doubt it was written down in the file in front of him. Then he asked me my age, my profession. He asked about my family, my siblings, and their work. He repeated the same questions they'd asked me at the first interrogation.

I assumed he was in the process of closing my casefile. He was doing everything my friend had enumerated when I asked her how one could figure out that their case was being closed. All those endlessly repeated questions that took about half a day to answer. Finally, he ordered me to be returned to my cell. After the door was locked, one of my cellmates asked me, "Surely he's going to close your case now?"

"Yes."

I told her what had happened and the questions he'd asked me. Then barely thirty minutes later, I was taken back to the interrogation room once again. This was to follow up with closing my file. Hours passed—I couldn't tell how many. I felt my tongue go dry in my throat. I asked for water. The interrogator brought me a cup, held it to my mouth, and ordered me to hold it. He lifted the bag from around my mouth a bit, so I could drink.

But the cup smelled of alcohol, so I didn't drink from it. He asked me sharply, "Why aren't you drinking? Didn't you ask for water? Take this." But I refused again, because I was afraid that he'd slipped something other than water into the cup. I didn't drink it, though I desperately needed a drop of water. My mouth had gone completely dry.

This case-closing process continued until the end of the second half of the day. I returned to my cell and told my cellmates what had happened this time. My friend Z.A. confirmed that this is how cases were closed. I asked her if this meant that I wouldn't be called back to interrogation again. "Not unless something new happens," she said. "Like if one of your friends informs on you or confesses something new about you. Or if someone from your town is arrested who knows something about you."

All that mattered was that my case be closed. Everything else was up to God's will—if I would be released or if I would die and be buried here. Our days were so monotonous, it felt like they all just blended into each other. My hope for imminent release began to wane. The only relief we got, the only moments during which we didn't feel trapped within the four walls of the prison, were the ten, or at the very most fifteen minutes we would spend in front of the cell door looking up at the sun, most often right after we'd gotten out of the shower. In these moments, we used to comb our hair, using the specific combs for prisoners that family members used to send us. The guards stored these combs for us and didn't let us bring them into our cells.

There was a large courtyard in front of the cells, at the center of which were beds for planting. There were some pine trees in them, but as soon as they grew, the guards would cut them down, as if they wanted to prevent us from having anything that could possibly make us breathe more easily. Then they built a new prison for women where the trees should have stood. The cell that got the best sunshine during the day was the one that got it at lunch time, and we nicknamed it the "tanning salon." At that time of day, the kilfa would come. We would suddenly spot some of the male prisoners in their navy-blue uniforms, the sound of their unvanquished footsteps advancing. You'd never guess they were only clad in plastic flip flops. For a quick moment, it would feel like you were seeing your own brother, and you'd get the urge to kiss him and ask him how he was doing. But then the voice of the prison guard would spoil this as he called out to his female colleague, "Guard!"

The female guard would hurry to usher us back into our cells, since the male prisoners were forbidden from seeing the female prisoners, and vice versa. And it was not only the men we didn't have the right to see, but even our female comrades in the adjoining cells. If it ever so happened that people from two cells were outside at the same time—like one was in the bathroom and the other was cleaning—the guards would disperse themselves among us so as to prevent us from seeing each other properly. The female guards did this even though they knew that their actions didn't ever preclude us from seeing each other through the holes in the windows or from under the doors, which we pulled tightly from the inside so we could see through to the outside. There was also a constant stream of conversation through the windows. They deliberately tried to prevent us from doing all of this, and also from seeing nature, so they placed Zinsco panels to obscure what we could see, only allowing a view of things that were a few centimeters away. But none of this prevented us from talking and passing messages from cell to cell.

Slow, bitter days rolled by. I spent many weeks in Cell Four. One day, the guard opened the door and asked me to gather my things and follow her. Whenever this happened, any prisoner—male or female—would anticipate their release. Perhaps it signaled release and freedom, but then again, the guards could just be moving prisoners from one cell to another. As it turned out, it was the second option. After removing me from my cell, the guard stopped in front of Cell Three, which was next door to Cell Four, opened it, and ordered me inside. She locked it once again.

New, pallid faces were looking at me for the first time, like ghosts risen from their graves. Three prisoners greeted me with thin smiles. We said hello with kisses on two cheeks and introduced ourselves by name. One of them promptly started notifying the rest of the cells what was happening. Something new—Nawal has been moved to our cell. We heard a voice coming from another cell, "Who took her place then?" "Let's ask Four," she replied, meaning the women in Cell Four. They'd ask them to find out who had taken my place.

This was routine procedure that happened from time to time, but it broke up the boredom—a new face, some news from outside. The person who had been busy communicating with the other cells joined our discussion, and we all had a long conversation. We had so many things to ask each other. They asked me about my case, the reason for my arrest, what was happening on the outside, if there was any news about an imminent release of prisoners. There were so many questions we wanted answers to, most of them revolving around the prison, male and female prisoners both, and especially the length of prison stays.

One prisoner, M.J., was very funny: she seemed to be in good health, but her skin was sallow and pale. She explained to me that she was "pudgy" because of a medication she took. But do they even treat people who get sick here? They barely give you a single painkiller if you're ill, and if your condition worsens, they just follow this up with a smile, meaning you're on the verge of death. They might transfer someone to hospital, but only after intense protestations from that prisoner's friends and comrades.

I asked my new cellmates how long each of them had been here. All their answers ranged from two to nine months. M.J. told me that she had been in prison for nine months already, and three months ago they'd brought in her father. "Your father is in here? How did you find out?" I asked.

"From the male prisoners."

"Can you speak to them?"

"No, but there is a way to find out what's going on over there. You'll learn how to soon enough."

She didn't really elaborate on her methods at first, but then she continued, "You'll learn tomorrow morning."

"But how?"

"When the door opens in the morning for cleaning, one of us stays in the cell and takes care of the actual cleaning while the others go to the bathroom, accompanied by the guard. The second guard stays behind with the person doing the cleaning, but she stands outside the cell, and sometimes not right in front of the door. Meanwhile, the male prisoners know when our cleaning time begins and when the doors are opened, so when the time comes, one of them peers out of the small window at the top of their cell." Our prison was located directly across from the men's Prison Four, and their cell windows were opposite the doors of our cells—only a few meters separated us. This all ended, however, when the new women's prison was built. This changed our process a little: when cleaning time came, the prisoner who stayed behind in the cell while the others were in the bathroom would hang out a piece of black cloth with a summary of our news written on it with soap. A male prisoner would read it by standing on his cellmates' shoulders. They would then respond to our questions in the same way, while keeping all this concealed from the guards. My God, despite all the material and human barriers between us, they were never able to prevent us from communicating with our brothers in our own ways.

Because of the window conversations we managed to have in prison, I already knew my three new cellmates by name and voice before I ever got to see their faces. They were good-hearted girls and resistance militants in every sense of the word. The bitter torments of prison did not succeed in changing their beliefs and principles. I had a clear image of them from my friend Z.A. who had painted me a picture of all the long-time prisoners she'd shared a cell with. One of them, F.R., was from the village of Markaba.[18] She was extremely thin. When I first met her, she was silent, a deep sadness in her eyes. I asked her how she was doing. "I am the most idiotic prisoner here," she said. Her response caught me off guard. Surprised, I followed up, "Why would you say this about yourself?"

18    The village of Markaba is located in the district of Marjayoun, about 40 kilometers from Bint Jbeil. MA and MH.

"Listen to this. I'd been in prison for thirty days and I hadn't confessed to anything. I was about to be released because they hadn't found any evidence or information against me."

"How come they arrested you in the first place?"

"It was an attempt to cast suspicion upon me, but because I was so stupid, I confessed most of what I did thirty days later. It's all because of that traitor F.Y. When I heard I was getting released, I wrote my story on the walls of the cell so that every new prisoner could read it. Under this, I wrote a warning that no prisoner should ever confess to anything she hadn't been confronted and charged with." Then she paused and was silent again for some time. When she resumed, she said, "But now I try to tell myself that I'm no better than all these men here. I should share in the same torture and imprisonment they do; I no longer care when they will release me." Then she started joking around, which masked her misery and despair. In a small voice, she said, "I'm also engaged…." She said this like a little girl, her smile obscuring so many tragic tales.

I replied, "Wow, are you really? How long now? Where's your fiancé?" I had so many questions. She answered me first with a broad smile, and then she told me that she had been engaged for about a year. Her fiancé was travelling abroad within the Arab world and they had agreed that he would come back after about two years so they could tie the knot. Her smile turned bitter then. "Here I am now, celebrating my wedding." Her story moved me deeply and I fell silent for a while myself. They hadn't just put her body in jail but had also imprisoned her joy and happiness. But she told me that she'd found her true calling in the operations that she carried out against our ruthless, relentless enemy. She spoke in a barely audible voice, but the tone of violent revolution was transparent in every single word she uttered. I felt this from M.J. as well.

Suddenly we found ourselves talking about the heroic resistance operation from the day before, and how it had plunged the female guards into a state of fear and terror. I asked M.J. if it was true that every operation carried out against this enemy and their collaborators would cause them to torture the prisoners in retaliation.

"Who told you this?" she asked me, and I replied, "I always used to hear people say that before I got arrested. I also heard that any time they watched a fight on TV they would then go and act the same thing out on the prisoners."

With a smile, she told me that this wasn't true. She said that these operations actually made them feel more cowardly and do nothing, though perhaps they did do some of these things during interrogations. That's when another prisoner interrupted us to confirm that what she was saying was true. She'd heard this before her arrest from former prisoners who'd told her. She then added that this hadn't happened for a long time.

We talked a lot and shared our stories—it was our sole comfort in that cemetery we were living in.

M.J. couldn't read or write; she had to sound out the letters in words. She told me that she'd left school a long time ago and never finished the fourth grade, because she had to help her mother look after her younger siblings. They were farmers, and this kind of work requires a lot of labor and physical exertion. Her love of the land and deep sense of belonging to it shone through in everything she said. She was hoping to be released as soon as possible so she could go back and cultivate her land, while also looking after her little brother whom she'd left behind at only two years of age.

This cruel, unjust jail kept her bound up in a bottomless pit of anxiety. "But slowly, surely, we will no doubt return," she said, never giving up hope.

We were all suffering behind these deadly walls, every inch of which we'd come to memorize. But our groans only bounced off the walls and landed back on us.

I spent several days in Cell Three, and then they transferred me to Cell Six—the last room in the corridor next to the bathroom. Why this abrupt switch, I wondered?

In Cell Six, you feel completely isolated, not only from the other prisoners but from the rest of the prison itself. Maybe it's because the guards' room is located between this cell and the others. You could barely receive any news from the other prisoners' cells. If any sound came from your cell, the guards would bang loudly on your door and order you to quiet down or receive some form of severe punishment. I got to know new prisoners in this cell. There were three women in it, including N.A. who was from the town of Qantara.[19] She'd been there for about seven months.

Though I was meeting these three prisoners for the very first time, I somehow sensed a kind of friendship and love from them, a sort of mutual recognition. This bond of unity is what we'd derived from our situation and shared destiny. It was as if everyone here were the same person, no matter her religion, sect, or belonging, all because we had the same enemy. On my third day in Cell Six, something major happened. The door opened, and the guard came in and said, "You have a visitor." I felt my heart pound so rapidly and yet at the same time it dropped so quickly that I feared it would never beat again. The guard handed me a plastic bag with some clothes and the few belongings we were allowed to have in prison, then shut the door and left. Choking up, I said to my cellmates, "She said I have a visitor and just left. Where is this visitor? Who came to visit me?"

One of my cellmates told me that "a visitor" was what they called the bag of stuff that managed to make its way to a prisoner, seeing as no family member had come to visit any prisoner since April of 1988. She said that they very well might have forbidden family visits, which we later learned was true—the enemy had banned all visits by relatives. I started rummaging through the bag. There were clothes in it that I recognized—I even recognized the handwriting on the bag itself, it was that of my sister N. I started kissing the writing on the bag—my sister had written these words and touched this bag! This means that it really was true, she hadn't been arrested as they'd tried to trick me into believing. This brought me great joy mixed with painful sadness. It was a strange, contradictory feeling I couldn't explain. I continued to look through my things. There was a bar of soap that I just stared at and

---

19    The village of Qantara is located in the Marjayoun district, about 26 kilometers from Bint Jbeil. MA and MH.

then suddenly, I cried out mirthfully, "Look everyone! There's a message carved into this bar of soap. 'We are doing fine.' Oh, thank God." You are so wonderful my sister, just these words from you have made me incredibly happy. Well done for thinking of this. There was also a box of tissues and a pair of slippers, which my cellmate took and stared at for a long time before suddenly shouting out, "Look, there are more words written here! They're tiny, you can barely make them out!" I picked them up eagerly and began examining the words carefully. It was the names of my siblings. I started kissing their names, tears sliding down my cheeks. My cellmates started crying when they saw how moved I was.

There was also a box of sanitary pads. When I saw those, I paused for a moment, lost in thought. My cellmates asked me what was wrong, why I'd grown so silent. I replied, "I didn't even notice…" They asked me what I was talking about.

"I have been in prison now for nearly two and a half months, but I haven't gotten my period at all—why?"

One of the young women replied, "Don't worry, so many other women here are in the same boat. Some didn't get their periods for four, five, even six months. It might be psychological, or it might be caused by the electric shocks. But don't worry, you'll get it again. You're lucky you didn't get it when you were first brought in and locked up in solitary confinement!"

"Why?"

"Because you wouldn't have known what to do! Especially in that situation. It happened to me." I asked her how she'd managed. "I didn't know how to react and eventually told the guard. She brought me a roll of toilet paper that I could use instead of a sanitary pad."

"And then what?" I asked.

"After that, I used toilet paper and the sanitary pads the other girls who'd gotten here before me gave me… until I got my own stuff. If we need pads and have some money in the safe, we're allowed to ask the guards to buy them for us. We can also ask for shampoo, underwear, tissues, soap, and a comb. But that's all we're allowed to purchase."

After my cellmate explained all these new things to me, I picked up the bar of soap and the slippers and started examining them anew. I was hoping I would find another bit of writing that would further reassure me about my family. But the words I'd already found were all there was. One of the girls then said to me, "Lucky for you, the guards didn't notice that. Any message from your family could cause a disaster for them and for you. No doubt your sister is aware of this and was very careful because the way she sent the message was extremely cautious and cannot be easily detected. The guards search everything that comes in for the prisoners and they confiscate anything that is not allowed." My mind went back to how these things could have actually made it to the prison. "But who brought these clothes? Could someone from my family have come here, but not been allowed to see me? Who could have possibly come other than my mother or sister?"

My friend answered, "When the guard opens the cell door at lunchtime, ask her. Maybe she knows." But would the guard really tell me?

I impatiently waited for lunch that day. When it finally came, I asked the guard who had brought my things here. She was called Samira, but her real name was Sayida. Sayida worked with her father in the prison, and she was the niece of the warden Jean Homsi, or Abu Nabil. She said that security had dropped off my things. I asked my friend what the guard meant by "security," and she replied, "It means an official from your town. There is a person from each town who comes here. Very often things are brought to us from our families by way of these "security" people. Perhaps someone from your family entrusted him with this because they were unable to come and visit you." This was an unusual day for me in prison. I was very happy to learn my family was alright. Even if the way I found out wasn't the most satisfying and hadn't really offered me any details about how they were actually doing, the most important thing was to know that they were generally all right.

Days passed, one after the other, with nothing new to report. All we heard were snippets of conversation exchanged between neighboring cells. And the few conversations we'd have with each other.

One day, the cell door opened outside of schedule, and an unfamiliar face appeared. It was a new prisoner. We'd heard from the other girls that she'd come about a week ago. She was the mother of two children—a nine-year-old boy and a six-year-old girl. I wondered why she'd been arrested. On our second day in the cell together, she started opening up to us. She said she was in her forties and had a job at the station where the collaborators worked in the evenings. She acted very cautiously around us. We could see questions swirling around in each other's eyes, as well as in the quiet whispers being exchanged. She noticed that we were reciprocating her cautious behavior.

That must have prompted her to justify why she'd been working at that kind of a place: she was a widow with difficult life circumstances and no other support at home. We didn't comment on her justification, but there was disapproval and censure in all of our eyes. But we still wondered why she'd been arrested. She hadn't done anything, according to her account. What made us even more cautious around her was the preferential treatment she was receiving from the guards. We limited our conversations with her to what it was like outside, how to make sweets, and new foods that she had been cooking at the station where the collaborators worked. I whispered into one of my cellmate's ears, "That stupid woman missed the perfect opportunity to poison them. It could've been a source of life-long pride for her. She's so stupid!"

Cell Six was the fourth stop for this woman who aroused our suspicion, especially as she'd not been tortured like the rest of the prisoners. She didn't stay with us for long and was moved back and forth between several other cells. About a month and a half later, she was released without anyone ever knowing the real reason for her arrest. The days passed, dull and boring. You hear screaming in the cell next door, intense banging on the iron window frame in another cell; the anxiety of being confined explodes in curses of rage, hatred, and revenge when prisoners are made to live in these circumstances.

I found myself in such a situation not long afterwards. Every prisoner, male and female, is bound to go through this at a certain point. I was still being transferred from one cell to another, a routine procedure that happened every so often. This time they brought me back to Cell Three. I'd been kept in it before, for several days. There were familiar faces there. We hugged as if I were returning from a journey in a faraway land, and we started asking each other questions about how we were doing, how each other's health was, and so on. After being transferred out of Cell Six, I felt like life was flowing once again. Everyone knew how isolated Cell Six felt. The people in there rarely know what's going on around them, whereas in the rest of the cells, you still manage to feel like you're in constant contact with the other female prisoners—and even the male prisoners, to some extent.

We resumed our conversations and our lethargy; we spent our days in deadly boredom. Most of the time, we just paced up and down the cell, either collectively or separately, reviewing what had happened to us or perhaps only in an effort to be alone with our own thoughts. Sometimes I passed the time by counting in my head while my friends were asleep. When I couldn't sleep, I would get up and walk up and down, counting each footstep. I would do this for about an hour, counting from one to sixty every minute.

No doubt every prisoner knew exactly how many tiles were on their cell floor, in length and width. You'd start to forget—or at least try to forget—what happened to you during the hours of interrogation you suffered before your file was closed. And then, the more time passes, all events of life in prison become routine and boring. Our externally imposed lifestyle in the prison system and our monotonous daily routine became the only things we expected. You get enmeshed in this lethal cycle—it's as if your life is none of your business, as if it isn't even your own life, as if your life stopped the moment you entered prison. All of this is normalized. Your days all run together in one long, endless stretch. Inside prison, trivial and inconsequential matters turn into big surprises.

Whenever simple things happen, things that are just part of the way life goes in this graveyard—like greeting a new guest and asking her about herself—it takes you right back to your own interrogation. You then automatically become the expert in these matters, which allows you to educate and warn the new prisoner about how things could go wrong. You try to raise her spirits and urge her to endure things with patience—you pass on the lessons you've learned from having been interrogated yourself. Another thing is the two-day rotation of the guards' work schedules. One group comes and the other goes. Sometimes there is a new face, a new guard who would have come to take the place of a former one. They may deliberately bring someone harsher, or maybe even someone softer, but at the end of the day, they are all collaborators and traitors to their country and their people.

All of these tiny little matters become the events you anticipate and spend all your time waiting for. It almost starts to feel like you were born in this prison, and it becomes ever more impossible to find any purpose in life. You become certain that you will die here. These thoughts dominate you and drive you to the point of despair. And then, just when you're on the verge of exploding, somehow your cellmate does something that rubs you the wrong way, though she didn't mean to. Deep down, you know that you're all going through the same thing. You're all suffering. But still you explode over something banal: maybe one of your cellmates made a sudden movement, maybe you had a misunderstanding or disagreed about some facet of this lethal routine of life in the cell. You start screaming, you pound on the cell walls, doors, and window with your fists or even your head. You might slap yourself on the face to the point where you sometimes hurt yourself without even realizing it. Your cellmates hold you back and try to stop this behavior. They're no stranger to these outbursts. They've experienced them themselves, maybe they still do...

Then, all at once, you feel ashamed. Even in prison, you resist. But is this not to be expected? You're a resistance fighter, after all; you sacrifice and move forward without hesitation or wanting anything in return. You regret having troubled your cellmates, but you couldn't stop yourself. You swear and curse the situation you are in, and then those very cellmates sit you down like some broken thing—but, in reality, you're just too ashamed and afraid to look at them. They did nothing to deserve the toxic atmosphere you'd just created.

Later, when you're calm again, you apologize for what happened and try to justify your behavior. It's the anxiety caused by confinement and the deadly boring life that passes with lethal languor here. You repeat your apologies and voice your regrets, perhaps you embrace and kiss your cell-mates, and, embarrassed, reiterate how sorry you are for what happened. You cannot allow your relationships inside the cell to become strained or your comrades will grow sick of you and your psychological state. But on some level, you know this could never happen: everyone here is fully aware and conscious of the life we're being subjected to. They all know that what you're suffering from is psychological in nature. They know where it comes from. The cramped cells, mistreatment by the guards, their attempts to sow mistrust between the prisoners: all these things add to the deadliness of our routine. Not to mention the malnutrition, the isolation from the outside world—you're totally cut off from everything related to your life outside, most importantly your family. You have no idea how they are doing. All of this is compounded by the insults you're constantly subjected to. If you're not insulted by their words, then you'll be insulted by the work you're required to do, like cleaning the guards' bathrooms.

You know that this enemy and their collaborators are very consciously and carefully denying you any form of comfort or reassurance. You know all this, and you know exactly where they're trying to take you, but sometimes it gets to be too much and you just lose control. Control of yourself, of your thoughts, of your nerves. And you need to find some way to relieve all this mental and physical stress, relieve your tense nerves and torment. But around every corner of your utter despair, are your cellmates, faithfully lying in wait, consciously holding you together with their stamina and immeasurable love. Yes, you exploded, but each of your comrades and cellmates will one day explode, too. This could happen at any moment, and then your turn will come to calm her down with your own awareness and reciprocal love.

In the midst of all this, the most important thing is that the guards not notice these nervous breakdowns. Witnessing them only makes them happy. Their goal is to destroy us, to make us fight with each other. They do not know that at the end of the day we are stronger than all of this. Hiding our weaknesses and breakdowns is a form of resistance against our malevolent jailers. We will not allow them to insult us, nor will we appear weak before them, no matter the reason.

You become increasingly attached to your friends who support you in prison because they are the only outlet for you to expose your weaknesses, the only people in front of whom you can allow yourself to collapse. These eventual collapses are the only way to preserve some psychological stability, which is the thing you need the most when you're stuck in prison. After you let it all out, things go back to normal, as if nothing ever happened. Voices from neighboring cells comfort you and try to calm you down and raise your spirits. Then you feel guilty: what about those who've been here for many more years than you? All of those male prisoners, what about them? Guilt turns to embarrassment and shame, and very quickly you come back to your senses. You then deliberately change the subject and delude yourself and everyone else into believing that inevitable liberation is soon to come.

Conversation becomes a preferred way to escape this bitter reality; it lets us travel to the outside world and what's happening there. When we let it halt for a while, each of us returns to her own thoughts and spends some time alone with them. We then resume conversation with someone or other, and things continue on at the same pace. Life here is so strange, how you slowly become a part of this place. You stop caring about it all—the deprivation, the torture, the sound of handcuffs that once terrified you, the bag over your head preventing you from seeing a thing. This all morphs into a memory that you recount with a smile on your face. You narrate your interrogation as if you were telling a story, or a funny joke. Maybe you even go further than that. You've completely evolved: you've become an actor—a comedian even—performing with your cellmates. One of them plays the part of the prisoner, another that of the interrogator, the third is the guard. We put a piece of someone's clothing over the head of the person acting out the role of the prisoner. It stands in for the bag. We use some other clothing to stand in for handcuffs, and we burst out laughing.

We keep taking this play one step further. Our voices get louder—especially that of the person playing the interrogator. But soon enough our game is brought to an abrupt halt with the sound of loud banging on the cell door. The guards are here, preventing us even from amusing ourselves. They hear our voices and no doubt they are surveilling what we are saying. They're eavesdropping. But even this distracting game begins to bore us. We search for new ways to kill the endless time stretching out before us before it kills us. Don't they say that necessity is the mother of invention?

You get involved in the very heart of the activities you come up with. We all do this to combat boredom because we must create something. They prevent us from entertaining ourselves or doing anything that would somehow allow us access to the outside world; we are allowed no newspapers, no magazines, no books, no radio, or anything that might bring some relief. This is all deliberate. They do not even allow any humanitarian organization—specifically the International Red Cross in our case—to contact us or check on our condition. You're forbidden from doing anything that would help kill the time. But you continue to resist while you are in prison. You plunge into the resistance against boredom and the endless time stretching out before you. You have to create something.

There are female prisoners who made beautiful handicrafts through which they expressed their hidden feelings and longing for their families and freedom. These crafts expressed their resistance against our tyrannical enemy. There are paintings executed with creativity and artistry, prayer beads dedicated to remembering loved ones and families. These artistic creations carry hundreds of beautiful meanings. But how could we make art, really, what materials could we use? There were some available, but in order to know how to use them, we had to learn from the prisoners who'd been there longer than us. We had to find out what they used to start creating their art.

The first craft is a string of prayer beads made of olive pits. Olives were readily available, as usually a few would come with breakfast. Every prisoner has copious stories about these olive pits which she subsisted on and used to kill time. You could use them to craft a gift for your family and loved ones, by making them into beautiful shapes of different colors. You begin by filing down both ends of the olive pit evenly, until you reach the core of the pit. You empty it out. Then you flatten its sides to make it even. Filing down the pit like this takes about five minutes. If you're planning to make a string of prayer beads, then you have to count the number of pits you have and continue to work out the math. The equation is as follows: if you need thirty-three beads and each bead takes about five minutes, you will kill about one hundred sixty-five minutes of your time in prison. This can add up to long hours. You then measure each pit a second time, so you have a good number of evenly shaped beads. This is the first step in making a string of prayer beads. Our fingers used to hurt so much from the sheer amount of time we spent filing with a pumice stone we found in our cell—or sometimes we would file it down with the edge of the window. We developed our craft. Next, we started giving the beads a color of our choice or one suggested by our cellmates. You also needed to thread a thin string through the hollowed-out olive pit by using a needle. But how could we get our hands on any needles?

There were so many anecdotes about the needle we used. It was made out of the tooth of a comb that we had filed down on the sides, to make it thinner. We then pierced a hole in it with the tip of a small nail we removed from a shoe. But this type of needle wore out quickly, and we really needed something more effective. We managed to turn some electrical wire, which we'd removed from inside the guards' bathroom, into an almost normal needle. But with such frequent use, even this needle began to bend—almost as if it had grown tired of its work. And all of this after we'd spent about thirty minutes or so making it!

This copper needle sometimes took on a reddish tint because of the blood that would seep from our fingers as they rubbed against it while we filed it. It became tricky to do this work so regularly, so we had to find a way to procure a regular needle that would allow us to work more consistently. A regular needle was allowed in, but the guards kept it and only allowed us to use it in case of necessity and for limited amounts of time. Sometimes even this regular needle would break and then we would have to inform the guards. They would order us to bury the two pieces of the broken needle in the dirt in the courtyard in front of our cell.

We were very determined to procure a regular needle. After long thought and many suggestions, we came up with something that we thought might work. At the time of day when the sun shone on our cell and the courtyard in front of it, we could secretly dig up the broken needles. A few days later, we would ask for a new needle to sew up a necessary item. Then after we got the good needle, we pretended to break it. We then handed over pieces of the old broken needle that we'd dug up and kept the new one. We brought this needle with us everywhere. It became the most precious thing we possessed, not just us personally but all of the prisoners in the cells around us.

The guards noticed that we were doing something inside our cells. Their spies in one of the cells watched what was going on in the rest. She waited for any news she could pass on to her masters, to be rewarded with a piece of chocolate or a few additional minutes outside her cell. We were then subjected to more searches by the guards who were trying to figure out what we could possibly be doing inside our cells. We knew what they were up to, though, and a code word would pass quickly from the cell next door warning us that our cell door might open at an unexpected time, or to stay in the cell for longer, or to let us know about a search to come.

The fate of those of us who were caught doing these handicrafts was to be locked in solitary confinement or have water poured over our heads. But they didn't know that this punishment only inspired us to create new things. Not to mention that we also exchanged these things between cells to share ideas about form and craftsmanship. With extremely limited means we were able to create a surprising array of crafts. Everything we touched carried the story of a vibrant, living resistance determined to overcome the worst circumstances.

## ON STRIKE: THE BEGINNING OF A PRISON UPRISING (EARLY AUGUST 1988)

The food that was given to the prisoners was barely enough to subsist on, just enough to survive. Often, we had to throw away entire meals because they were impossible to chew. It was like putting a block of cement into your mouth, if you can imagine that. Most meals were frozen into one solid block and only began to thaw after being put on our plates. This is what pushed many of us to ration our breakfasts and eat only a few olives in the morning, making the boiled eggs our lunch. The important thing was to stay alive and not collapse. The situation deteriorated as diseases ran rampant throughout the male and female prisoner populations due to malnutrition. That's when we decided to take action.

Breakfast had been distributed throughout the prison, and no sooner had lunchtime come than we heard proclamations coming from all the cells: "We are on a hunger strike and we will not take it anymore. You call this food? Even animals could not eat this."

All the cells responded to the call for the strike and the prisoners refused to eat anything until they improved the food. The guards threatened to report our behavior to the prison warden. This is what we wanted, so then they started dangling the punishments that awaited us before us. But none of us paid any attention to what they were saying. We needed to not back down or let our resolve weaken. Whatever was in store for us, how could it be worse than the state we were in?

We had demands and they needed to be met. These demands were not limited to improving our food. There were other important ones as well. The prisoners all agreed on one shared position after councils for each cell convened and came up with a unified decision: We would all take the same position of refusal when dinner was distributed. And that is what happened.

The guards repeated their threats and their anger escalated to the point that one of them rushed to bring in an interrogator. All he did was throw around blame and reprimands, threatening to punish us.

Anticipation filled the air. The interrogator entered one of the cells. Everyone was silent. You hold your breath, wondering what's happening in that cell. He threatened and cursed but the response was clear: We will not eat until our demands are met.

The next day, the cleaning began as usual, and everyone was in a state of rage. We did not back down. Breakfast was distributed and everyone refused to take it, except for the collaborators. Our anger at them intensified. The guards increased their threats, naming all types of punishments that we'd receive once the warden arrived. We resumed our observations and consultations. No doubt the prison warden would summon one or more of the women prisoners—together or individually—to find out what was going on. It was mere hours before this did indeed happen.

One of the prisoners was summoned. They handcuffed her, put the blindfold on and bag over her head, as if she was being led once again to interrogation. We all waited eagerly for her return, and about half an hour later she was sent back to her cell. Then a new prisoner was taken to the warden's office and we rushed to the windows to try to get a glimpse of what happened to her. The warden promised to convey our demands to the Israelis, since he didn't have any authority over the matters that we were protesting. He promised that there would be a reply from "them," i.e. the Israelis, but that for now we must end the strike, or we would be punished. He said that what we were doing would reflect badly upon us. He promised to have this resolved in a few days. This was the warden's official response to our strike.

We resumed consultations and conversations between the different prison cells, discussing what the warden had promised us. There were conflicting opinions about suspending or continuing the strike. In the end, we agreed to suspend the strike for a set period of time and if conditions didn't improve during that period, we would resort to an escalation in which we would refuse everything—even leaving our cells and taking showers.

The situation went back to how it had been and continued like that until August 22, 1988. Our first demand was met on that day—in the evening, we had our first dinner made of Lebanese products: a wedge of Picon cheese, a boiled egg, and tea. The quality of the food began to improve somewhat, but our other important demands were not met. An extremely important thing had happened; we had created a new atmosphere within our prison cells. This also helped to kill some time. They began distributing bags of lentils to each cell so we could sort and clean them, and they also gave us green beans to shell. We prepared these ingredients for the prison kitchen, for meals for our prison sisters and brothers.

The loveliest thing about this was that we could send messages or even very small things through the lentils and beans to our brothers in struggle. Their reply would come the following week. This was done with extreme caution, out of fear for our brothers. We didn't want anything to be discovered, so that none of them would be punished for it. On one occasion we received a number of brightly colored ribbons inside a bag of green beans. They were wrapped up neatly as evidence that our brother comrades had received what we'd been sending.

Days, weeks, months passed, and the year was about to come to a close. My mental and physical health had begun to decline, and my overall condition was deteriorating. This was not just true of me but was the same for many female prisoners, especially those who'd been arrested at the same time as me, over the same operation. I informed the guards about my condition and they promised to convey a message to the nurse who in turn promised to transfer me to hospital. But this didn't happen for a very long time, and it only did after numerous demands were made on my behalf by my imprisoned sisters in struggle.

At last, the day I had been promised for so long finally came. It was the first time I would be taken to the hospital. I wondered how I would be transferred there. The most important thing was that I was leaving this graveyard—even if just for a few hours. I asked my cellmates—especially those who knew about hospital visits—many questions. This was helpful because some of them had actually been taken to the hospital before. On the day I was scheduled to go, I was moved to the guards' room at around 9 AM. A nurse was waiting there and asked me about my condition. The way he was speaking to me made it clear that he was just making conversation; he didn't really care how anyone was doing or what was wrong with them—even if they were on the verge of death.

He asked the guard, "Are there any others?"

"Three more," she replied.

"And what's wrong with them?"

"Same as the others."

It was at that point that I figured out I wouldn't be the only one taken to the hospital. When everything was ready, they transferred us one by one to the ambulance—handcuffed and with bags over our heads the whole time.

I will never forget that moment. As soon as we boarded the ambulance, we all started whispering to one another, and then the surprise came! It makes sense that ill health brought us all together. K.Z., G.A., F.Y., and me: we were all there. All the prisoners who were arrested for the same operation as me, and we were all eagerly talking to each other. But the guard and nurse who were accompanying us warned against making any movements, including lifting the bags from our faces even a tiny bit. They sat us very close to each other on opposite sides of the ambulance. Then we started to step on each other's feet; we greeted each other by touching shoulders. The vehicle set off. We were leaving prison!

A strange feeling overwhelmed me, and I felt that I desperately needed to cry. No doubt we all felt this. It was as if we were going to see our families, toward the outside world and freedom. The vehicle started off down the road and during the journey, I heard a voice whispering, asking me about my health and how I was doing overall. It was K.Z. I knew it well. It was followed by the cough of a young man. My God, was there a male prisoner back here with us too? I wondered who he was and what was wrong with him. We couldn't find out anything about him. I began whispering back to K.Z. but the guard noticed and ordered us to remain silent. But we paid no attention and went back to whispering to each other in barely audible voices.

We arrived at the hospital, but we couldn't see anything. We heard a male guard order the people who were there to move away because we were going to pass through and go into the examination room.

After a little while, I found myself inside a room where the female guard told me to get up on the table. She sat down next to me but didn't take of the handcuffs or remove the bag from my head. I heard someone ask me how I was doing. This must be the doctor.

After a quick examination the doctor's response was: "It's nothing. It's psychological." Then he asked me if I'd been exposed to electric shocks. The nurse who'd come into the room with us intervened, "Please don't ask about anything outside your areas of specialization." The doctor then repeated what he'd said to me at first, "This is psychological and nothing to worry about. I'll write you a prescription for a ten-day treatment, and then they'll bring you back here."

When it was finished the guard led me to the waiting room, so the rest of the women could have their turn with the doctor. No doubt the same thing would happen to them. Then we finished up and went back to the prison the same way we came. The whispering resumed as we asked each other what the doctor had said. Our answers were all the same. We returned to the graveyard, each of us back to our own cell where our cellmates were waiting for us. They started asking us questions about everything that had happened. After only about an hour, the guard came back to ask me if I had any money being kept by the prison authorities. I responded in the negative. "Why? To buy medicine?" She replied, "It doesn't matter, when the security person responsible for your town comes, we'll give him the prescription to pass on to your family. They'll buy you the medicine and send it to you through him." Then she left without adding another word.

Her words hit me like a thunderbolt. I looked at my cellmates in shock and felt my heart squeeze tight in my chest. The room was spinning all around me. I involuntarily burst into tears, before I could realize what was happening. One of my cellmates asked me why I was crying.

"Didn't you hear her? My family will find out I'm not doing well, and they'll go nuts. This is terrible, how will they take it? No doubt they're deliberately trying to torture me and my family. I don't want medicine or anything else from them. All that matters to me is that my family never find out about this."

The next thing I knew, I was knocking on the door, "I want to see the guard." The door opened and she asked me what I wanted. I told her that I didn't want my family to know what had happened and I didn't want to send the prescription to them. I no longer needed the medicine. After I told her this, she replied, "This is for the warden to decide, we don't have anything to do with it." As usual she barked out her words quickly and succinctly and immediately left. My cellmates suggested that I meet the prison warden and ask him directly. I knocked on the cell door once again, and the guard answered me without opening it this time. I told her that I wanted to see the warden about an important matter, now if possible. She answered me, "Not now, maybe in the morning."

I stood at the window, mourning what had happened. I started banging my hands against the window's iron bars. Not fully conscious of my actions, I shouted the same phrase over and over again, "I'd rather they kill me than let my family know about this." My cellmates were trying to calm me down and ease me out of the state I was in. My companions in the cell next to mine asked me through the windows what had happened. My cellmates informed them what was going on, and at the same time the guard knocked on the door ordering me to lower my voice.

I became hysterical. I felt that my physical torture had been much easier to endure than this. I could withstand any torture, so long as my family didn't know about it. Darkness fell, and the next morning when the door opened at cleaning time, I asked the guard to inform the warden that I needed an urgent meeting. She promised she would. After about two hours, she came with just the bag for my head, brought me to his office, and left. A few moments later, I heard a voice order me to remove the bag from my head. I was now in the warden's office, sitting right across from him. He asked me why I had requested the meeting. I told him and pressed him not to tell my family anything. He promised me that he wouldn't. The meeting took no more than five minutes and I was brought back to my cell.

My friend K.Z. intervened, from inside her cell next door, to try to get me to calm down. She said that the women prisoners could pool their money and buy me the medicine. When I had the money, I could pay them back. She was in the same situation as I was, and so was G.A. It didn't matter to F.Y. because they—the people she was collaborating with and for—would cover the costs of whatever she wanted. About her I said, "May God never forgive her. She sold out and destroyed everything." All that mattered to me now is that they not inform my family about our situation.

A few days later, I secured the sum from the women prisoners and the medicine was delivered to me and my comrade. We started taking it according to the doctor's instructions, the guards administered it to us. About ten days passed, and then another week, but with no results. I asked my friends how they were feeling. I learned that G.A. was feeling better, but that for K.Z. nothing had changed. No one knew how F.Y. was doing because she didn't speak to the other women prisoners through the windows and refused to share a cell with anyone who did. She even used to stop anyone sharing a cell with her from doing so. She went so far as to complain to the guards and turn in anyone who talked through the windows. She would also snitch on them to the warden who had ordered punishment for anyone who spoke out against the prison authorities. Days passed, and then a month, and K.Z. started to feel better too, thank God.

But nothing changed for me. I didn't feel any better. I informed the guards again that the medicine wasn't working. During this period, I had been transferred to Cell Five. That's where I met prisoners whose faces were new to me but whose names and voices I knew very well. In that sense, they were at once strange and familiar. They'd been in prison a long time. We had a warm first meeting, as we'd been longing to meet each other face to face. We talked about all the usual things and about each cellmate's prison story.

Cell Five was next to the guards' room. It was different from the rest of the cells in that it had a window next to the door, though it was coated with dark paint which made it impossible to see through. The window was also a bit higher than usual, so the only way you could clearly look outside was to do so secretly, by climbing up on something. We were forbidden from opening this window except when cleaning the cell.

The position and location of this cell allowed us to monitor every-thing happening outside, and sometimes even to hear what was going on inside the guards' room. We could overhear some of their conversations. A number of times we were able to hear some bits of news reports when the television was turned up a little—especially at night. We did so by pulling on the bottom of the door forcefully, which somewhat helped the sound filter through so that we could make out some words more clearly. I spent most of my imprisonment in this cell; I was locked in it for one of the four years I spent in the Khiam Prison. Most of the major events that happened during my detention took place while I was in this cell. The most important of these were my "visitors" from my family, every two weeks. "Visitors" were the things that families sent to the prisoners. These were either delivered through the security official or in person by a family member. Relatives would arrive at the prison gates, knowing that their loved ones were right inside, but they wouldn't find out until long afterwards whether their deliveries were received by their rightful recipients.

What a painful situation. You are separated from your loved ones by only a few meters, but, in reality, you are separated by months, years even. This leaves a lump in your throat and a tightness in your chest. A feeling of bitterness lingers. They can't see you, but there's nothing stopping them from imagining what you must look like now. Once strong, healthy, and well-cared for, you are now pale, thin, and humiliated. You imagine what they look like too: you conjure up an image of each member of your family, and they all appear to be just the way you left them. Your last memory of them is still stuck in your head. Days, months, years pass by and this image never changes... except maybe sometimes, fading away a little, fraying at the edges.

You can't make sense of this situation; it persists year after year. The lump in your throat gets bigger, your heart hurts until it feels like it is only beating with longing to see and embrace your family once more. This gets so intense that you spend innumerable hours just thinking about the moment when you will see them again. You make a pledge to yourself that after your release you will never leave them again—not even for a single moment. Then you are jolted out of all this daydreaming back to your painful, deadly reality.

Imprisonment becomes increasingly awful; different diseases spread among the male and female prison populations. Their painful screaming rings in our ears. One prisoner could no longer see clearly. It was suggested that G.A. meet the warden and ask that her family be allowed to send glasses with prescription lenses to her. She wore them even before she was arrested, but now they're no longer strong enough to correct her worsening vision. After several requests by us and her, she was seen by the doctor and he prescribed new lenses for her family to send to her. This kind of situation is tragic, not only for the individual prisoner, but also for their families who become preoccupied with terrible thoughts about the fate of their children in prison. The family then wonders: What's happened to our daughter? She must be losing her eyesight or else they wouldn't have asked us to send her new glasses.

This is a simple case compared to others. Skin conditions, especially eczema, afflicted many female prisoners. Can you imagine someone scratching their skin off until it bled? This is what happened to many people who contracted this disease. K.Z. and K.A. both got it, along with many other prisoners. We made urgent demands to get treatment for this disease that was destroying our skin, even if the treatment was at our own expense, and even if it meant calling in a doctor specialized in skin conditions.

Their answer: We need to ask the Israeli leadership if they will allow it.

How can we be cured of an illness like this when everything around us encourages its spread? Lack of sun, air, and food, as well as poor medical attention, which in prison amounts to nothing more than basic first aid. The condition of two female prisoners worsened to the point that they had to be completely isolated from the rest of us. Is what happened to them not enough to warrant a specialized doctor? One of them also suffered from acute rheumatism; of the many others like her, few survive. Many diseases and conditions needed treatments, but we had to remain strong and deal with these things ourselves. We had to endure and never weaken or despair. We had to fight these illnesses with all our patience and resilience.

One afternoon, we heard a cell door open, which either meant that someone had been transferred to solitary confinement or that someone new had been arrested. It took us a few moments to be able to gather what was going on. Two new young women had been arrested. The information we received indicated that they were from the town of Aramta.[20] One of them was in her forties and disabled. I wondered what was wrong with her and what her story was. The prison's communication network went into action. To activate it, all you had to do was hit the wall of the cell next to yours three times and if you heard a cough at the window of the cell you were trying to reach, it meant that the coast was clear and you could talk.

We started with questions about the two new women. Some preliminary information was available: names, town, where they'd been put. If you felt there was an emergency, like the guards were banging on your door and might raid your cell, you had to stop talking and inform the person you were speaking to so that she could avoid punishment or reprimand. You closed down communication with the following words, "Pass it, pass it around, give me a drag before she comes, before the guard comes!"[21] You would repeat this several times, pretending to actually be singing, so as not to arouse the guard's suspicion, and then you'd go back

---

20   Aramta is located in the Jezzine district, about 55 kilometers from Bint Jbeil. MA and MH.

21   This is a play on the René Bendali song, *Pass it Around*: "Pass it, pass it around, let me get a drag before the police comes." MA and MH.

to observing the situation outside your cell door. If there was no longer anyone there, you could contact the other prisoners in the adjacent cell again. This method of communication worked for all of the cells, except for the ones housing the collaborators. They had specific cells assigned to them. This included Cell One where F.Y. was, and Cell Two where I.I. stayed. She was from the village of Deir Siriane and also collaborated with the interrogators inside the prison.[22] So these two cells were reserved for female collaborators and informers.

We were all asking the same question: How is this woman doing? She is disabled, so is she all right? We didn't really find out until after she was transferred to be with the other prisoners. They said she was a lot of fun, and a sister in struggle. She had been attempting to undertake a daring operation, but had aroused suspicion and was caught. I longed to get to know her but didn't get the chance to until she was arrested for a second time, only a week after her release. She'd been released after being in prison for eight months, but she spent less than one week out before they arrested her again. She was brought to the cell I was in. It was a huge shock for her and for us. How terrifying she looked—she was nearly unconscious. It was an unreal nightmare for her to be back in this cemetery again. She couldn't believe that she'd been given a new lease on life but then too soon was as good as dead and buried once again. Perhaps they'd deliberately released her for that short period so she would discover and be tormented by her father's death. After she was released, she'd been forbidden from leaving her town. That's what she told us after she caught her breath and the nurse who'd been called to relieve her shock gave her a sedative to calm her nerves. She wasn't the only person to be rearrested; many male and female prisoners were rearrested only shortly after their release.

A new Eid was approaching, and with it, new hope for our release. Perhaps a number of prisoners might be liberated this time. But our hopes were dashed just as they'd been during Eid al-Fitr. On the morning of the

---

22    The village of Deir Siriane is in the Marjayoun district, about 31 kilometers from Bint Jbeil. MA and MH.

Eid everyone was in a state of high anticipation. We stood at the windows, wishing that God would return all of the prisoners to the warm embrace of their families and loved ones. But, as usual, we were in for disappointment.

Many of us developed nervous conditions. It was a reaction to the continuous disappointment we had to endure. The prisoners' families all expected their children to come home for Eid, and my family was no exception. But the Eid was upon us once again. And prisoners are not with their loved ones…[23] There was nothing new to report except an increase in the gloom and despair looming over everyone. I had a very intense attack of nerves when I realized that my release had become an unattainable dream, and that seeing my family and loved ones would be impossible.

Days passed and the nights of Ashoura arrived. We always used to commemorate them by talking about the misfortunes suffered by the Prophet Muhammad's grandson Husayn. Anyone who knew the stories about the Prophet and his family would share them by holding discussions or staging funerals and mourning sessions in which people who had the skill and talent would recite the Qur'an. This used to bother the guards who forbade us from holding these sessions whenever they heard us convening them.

Days and then seasons passed. Autumn approached, dampening our spirits and making us feel gloomy. Our daily rhythms grew boring. We had exhausted all topics of conversation. But we had to overcome this feeling and find a new way of living, enter a new phase of prison reality that was now centered on the exchange of facts and information. Anyone who had some kind of knowledge would teach the others. I learned how to do some physical exercise routines from a prisoner who was really good at it. But she didn't stay in prison long. She was from the town of Hebbariye and was arrested with her sister.[24] She was arrested on suspicion of aiding the resistance, and as a result of torture she invented things that had never happened. She felt compelled to invent a false story

---

23  This is a line from a poem by the famous classical Arabic poet, al-Mutanabbi. MA and MH.

24  The town of Hebbariye is in the district of Hasbaya, about 56 kilometers from Bint Jbeil. MA and MH.

under interrogation just to make the torture stop. After her interrogation ended, they put her with the other prisoners. Then they started moving her from cell to cell. When she was put in ours, I learned these exercises from her and practiced until I'd mastered them. I started doing them daily for the rest of the time I was in prison, and eventually even began teaching them to my comrades who were transferred into my cell.

Upon our insistence, this prisoner confessed to the warden that she'd invented a false story. His response was to put her in solitary confinement for three days. She was returned to the cells, but she was then released less than three months after this incident.

I developed a specific schedule for myself that helped me kill the long hours in prison: performing all the additional prayers you can do according to Shia rituals, exercising with others who also liked to work out, and making handicrafts.

It was the month of October 1988. We were exchanging snippets of conversation as usual one evening; it was about 8 PM. We heard the television being switched on in the guards' room, which shared a wall with our cell. The sound was intermittent, but it was an opportunity for us to hear some bits of news, it didn't matter what kind. I rushed and pulled hard against the bottom of the door after laying on the ground and pressing my ears against its iron frame. I couldn't hear clearly. A few moments later, I suddenly screamed, "Listen!!" No one moved a muscle or even breathed. I held my breath. Oh God, what was I hearing? I jumped up like someone who'd just heard news of her own release. Everyone asked me, astonished, "What? What is it?!"

"They assassinated Lahad!"[25]

"How do you know?"

"I heard the news just now. He was assassinated by a brave woman called Sonya!" (This is how I heard her name at the time, but we later learned that her name was Soha Bechara.) "He is now in an Israeli hospital. This is the best news I've ever heard!"

---

25  Antoine Lahad (1927-2015) was the leader of the South Lebanese Army (SLA). MA and MH.

The prisoners had so many questions. They tried to dampen my excitement so I could speak more coherently. "Tell us everything you heard in detail."

"I was able to make out that it was a girl from Deir Mimas.[26] She was called Sonya, I think, but I couldn't hear her family name. She attempted to assassinate the collaborator and agent Antoine Lahad. He is in critical condition and has been transferred to a hospital inside Israel."

A few moments later one of the prisoners used our communication system to convey the good news around the prison. Conversations started at all of the windows. Everyone wanted to talk about this; a feeling of joy pervaded all of the cells. We prayed to God that the male prisoners had heard the news as well but, in any case, we would inform them the following day.

Cautious and careful window-side conversations continued in code, so that none of the guards or police officers near our cells could understand what we were talking about if they heard us. Suddenly they turned out the lights. It wasn't the scheduled time yet, but they did so anyway. No matter! Something important had happened and no doubt many things would change. Things would surely be clearer tomorrow. What a lovely night we had, discussing all of our hopes that these kinds of operations would keep recurring day after day.[27]

When morning broke, the guards didn't come and open our doors according to schedule. This was the first clue that something important had happened. There were unusual movements outside, and we heard the guards' footsteps coming and going. Two hours passed and there had been no cleaning, no distribution of breakfast, not even an opportunity for us to empty our makeshift toilets. We desperately needed water. We started knocking on the cell doors, asking to go to the bathroom and fill up our water, but they didn't let us out.

---

26    Deir Mimas is a town in the Marjayoun district, about 36 kilometers from Bint Jbeil. MA and MH.

27    On November 17, the communist militant activist Soha Bechara attempted to assassinate Antoine Lahad. SLA agents later admitted that this action precipitated Israel's withdrawal from occupied South Lebanon. MA and MH.

"Didn't I tell you that all I heard was true? You doubted it when I told you the news," I said to my cellmates. I was certain that I hadn't misheard. Lunchtime came. We didn't hear the sounds of the kilfa of male prisoners calling out to the guard. We waited for this sound every day, three times a day—or sometimes more—because it meant that our beloved brothers, the male prisoners were near. We tried hard to see their faces through the tiny holes in our windows or under the door. Sometimes we were able to exchange furtive whispers with them. At others, we would say things in loud voices, meaning for them to hear. We might sing a song that the women had composed for the male prisoners, like one that went like this: "Hey Mr. Blue Uniform, you with that shovel and towel, I'm singing this song for you, Mr. Prisoner." Someone would sing this while I peered under the door to catch a glimpse of one of them. I turned to my friends to tell them I'd seen one of their faces—that is one of the male prisoners—and that he looked at the door and smiled. My cellmates then also tried to see under the door, each one of them rushed over to see if it were her blood brother.

Some time after the supposed lunch distribution, we finally heard the sound of the kilfa. The men were bringing the food. Would the doors be opened? We waited. A little bit later, we heard the sound of the door opening in Cell Six—we knew what each door opening sounded like and could distinguish them from one another. Each door made a slightly different sound when it was opened. Our turn came. The guard ordered us to take the food, but she also ordered that only one of us do it—though usually we picked up our food as a group. She warned us not to come near the door. We told her we needed to fill up our drinking water, but she refused, saying we could do it according to schedule, when we went out to the bathroom at dinner time. All of these things that were going on only seemed to confirm that the news we'd heard was indeed true. No doubt whoever had carried out this assassination attempt was now here in prison with us. Otherwise why would they be so tough on us? The guards looked at us with eyes filled with hatred and loathing, and the way they spoke to us was just as disparaging.

None of us could ask why we'd been under siege from the early morning on. They thought we knew nothing, but we all knew what had happened. They were so stupid! They didn't know that despite their blockade, locking us in and acting so tough, we knew everything that was happening around us. Thanks to the Creator who gave us the ability to hear—the most important sense a prisoner could possess: it stands in for all the rest of the senses and with time develops to be very acute. When dinnertime came, we heard the voice of one of our bothers calling out, "Hey guard!" Often, we repeated this after him from inside our cells, making a word play in Arabic, changing just one letter to say, "Hey stupid," our own way of referring to the guards. We all got ready to leave our cells; perhaps we would be able to find out something new that would further clarify what we'd heard.

The door opened. One of us took the dinner trays while my other cellmate and I picked up the big container to fill it with water. We headed for the bathroom. But the guard escorting us shouted right in our faces, "Not here, the other bathroom!" She meant the bathroom next to Cell Six, which was used by the guards. The usual bathroom for female prisoners was located at the end of the corridor opposite Cell Seven, which we called "the Dungeon." We did what we were asked to do. The guards ordered us to speed up and work faster. Once we finished, we returned to our cells and the doors were locked on us again. At that point we really started talking about the importance of this event, in light of the procedures that they were putting in place and what they could still do in the coming days. The next day, our daily work routine returned to normal, but the guards were very cautious around us. Through our window communications network, one of our fellow prisoners informed us that she'd heard one of the guards talking to the other saying, "Alia, she's so cruel! She didn't even shed one tear. You should have seen her laugh! She doesn't care about anything." Alia is the pseudonym of one of the guards; her real name is Afaf and she is from the town of Marjayoun. Her colleague is called Samira, but her real name is Sayida.

The new prisoner was put in Cell Seven, the dungeon or "the Hole." Every time we heard the sound of her cell door opening, which was clearly audible to all of our cells, we took our usual places from which we could see things outside. Indeed, we were then able to see the young woman whose name I'd heard on television. She was thin, medium height. She seemed brave and bold, from how she held her handcuffed hands out to how she raised her head high, unafraid of anything. But what kind of torture was in store for her?

We tried to watch her through every little opening in the cell door until she was transferred to cell one, which we used to call "Private School." That's where F.Y. was staying. During the time she spent in that cell, we were able to talk to her and learn more about her. Her name was Soha Bechara and she was from the town of Deir Mimas. Her name wasn't Sonya, as I'd thought I'd heard through the television static. She was the one who'd undertaken this heroic operation. The number of female prisoners increased greatly within days of this event. From an original count of twenty-nine prisoners, we now had forty-five within four or five days, most of whom were from the village of Hula[28] and belonged to the Communist Action Organization in Lebanon (OACL). These detentions were all in retaliation to the courageous operation Soha had undertaken. During this period, they also added more cells to the women's prison and made a number of changes. I was once again transferred to Cell Six. There were now eight women in this cell, and a similar number in the other cells. The reason for their arrests was all the same—all they had done was hang up posters praising Soha's heroic deed. But they wanted to know: Who did it?

The overcrowded conditions in the prison continued for about a month, but then the number of female prisoners began to decrease as some people were released. This was accompanied by some changes to the cells; I was transferred along with a number of others to Cell Five. My mental and physical health were worsening by the day because of the

---

28   Hula is a village located in the Marjayoun district, about 19 kilometers from Bint Jbeil. Zionist forces committed a massacre of innocent people there on 31 October 1948, killing more than 80 people. MA and MH.

interruption to my menstrual cycle. After having made several requests, I was once again transferred to hospital with another prisoner called R.J. She was sharing Cell One with F.Y. and Soha Bechara. On our way to the hospital, this prisoner passed a verbal message to me straight from Soha herself. She'd also given it to F.Y. and asked her to pass it on to me, not knowing if she'd actually do it or not. The message was about the meaning of resilience and endurance, that my condition was psychological, and I could overcome it.

After a while, Soha was transferred to Cell Six where she remained for about a month. During this period, she lent the prisoners strength, courage, and the ability to face up to our difficult circumstances. Later, Soha was returned to the dungeon of Cell Seven, where she remained for about a year, unable to move or even breathe.

## MARTYRS AND THE UPRISING

On the morning of November 25, 1989, we woke up to the sound of pounding on the doors. It was coming from Prison Four—the men's prison right across from the women's prison. This pounding was accompanied by protest chants of "Allahu Akbar." Their voices grew louder; the pounding and banging kept increasing until all the prisoners could hear it. We were in a state of panic: what was happening to the men? We rushed to the windows to try to find out. It seemed as if it was an uprising. It was our duty to stand in solidarity with our fellow prisoners, our brothers. Without giving it a thought, we started banging on the doors of our cells too, also shouting out protest chants and "Allahu Akbar."

As everyone's voices rose to a clamor, one of the female prisoners had a panic attack inside her cell. She kept crying out that they were torturing her brother. He was being held in Prison Four, and she was terrified that they were electrocuting him. We tried to ease her fear, re-assuring her that what was happening was an uprising by all the men in the prison. The shouts and banging continued to rise from every cell, so much so that the guards had to beat us back from the doors, demanding that we stay calm and threatening to bring in the interrogators to punish everyone. A few moments later there was the sound of an explosion that accelerated the pounding and shouting. This was a situation of deadly defiance. Then there was the sound of coughing, which reached us loud and clear. We heard voices demanding that a nurse be brought in. No doubt the prison guards had used a smoke bomb to quell the uprising, but this did not stop it.

Loudspeakers started calling for an end to the rioting, their voices clear. The response of our heroic prisoners was equally clear: "We want to meet with the Israeli officials in charge, we want our sick comrades to be released, and we want an improvement in our living conditions. We also want family visits." The voices making these demands were hoarse from smoke inhalation. The sound of the pounding on the cell doors at times got louder and at times dampened. None of the doors were ever opened. A state of high alert permeated the entire prison. A volcano of rage had erupted to destroy and put an end to all this injustice and deprivation. The loudspeakers were calling for calm.

"The warden wants to speak to you all." But the prisoners' voices were louder than the loudspeakers. They repeated their demands. The warden could only promise to convey these demands to the Israeli leadership as soon as possible. He wanted to be done with this uprising. The voices subsided by noon that day and quieted down a little, hoping that their demands would be met as soon as possible. Before sunset, we heard a young man shouting, and it seemed that it was coming from where the guards were stationed and not the interrogation rooms. We heard the sound once again, the pounding on the doors restarted, and we went back to participating in the uprising even more powerfully than before because now we were also protesting the torture of a number of our brothers whose wails and moans flooded our ears.

The guards then called in one of the interrogators. Our cell door was opened, and the interrogator entered cautiously, as if he were afraid of something—the guard walked behind him like a shadow. The guard did not utter a single word while the interrogator told us to stop what we were doing. "There's no point," he started saying and I interrupted, "So the screams that we heard from near the guard's station: what do those mean?" He shouted at me, "Don't interfere." I replied, "How are you telling me not to interfere when we can hear our brothers being tortured? Do you expect us to stay silent?" The other female prisoners echoed what I said, and he replied sharply, "If this continues, your fate will be the same as theirs—that's the punishment for people who participate in riots."

But I interrupted again, "How is demanding to be released, to have our living conditions improved, and to be able to see our families equivalent to taking part in a riot?" I cursed him in a whisper, and he quickly stated, "If you protest like this, it's a riot, and we'll punish you accordingly. You're better off if you stay calm. If you have demands, the prison warden is here, and you can make your demands to him—but not like this." He then repeated his threat that anyone who seeded chaos in the prison would be putting themselves at risk of the harshest of punishments. And then he left.

We heard banging and pounding on the walls of the cell next door. They wanted to know what had happened. The interrogator had entered only our cell and spoken only to us. We had to inform all the other cells what he'd said. Everyone started cursing him and his ilk loudly and clearly, purposely making themselves heard. We discussed the situation among ourselves, anticipating what would happen next. We took a collective decision to go on hunger strike until the situation had become clearer.

The next morning, we heard the sounds of shouting and banging on walls once again—this time from Prison One. But these sounds didn't last long, only a few hours, and then silence enveloped the prison. It seemed as if something had happened, but what? The doors opened for cleaning to begin as usual, but we refused to take our food. The same thing happened at lunchtime. When it was time for dinner to be distributed, one of the interrogators helped pass it out. It was the very first time that had happened. He started threatening us with severe punishments. We paid no mind to his threats. He went back to his old tactics, telling us that everything would be fine, but that change would only come through discussions with prison officials—not by a strike or any other action. But we collectively refused. We wouldn't take any food until things had been clarified. He departed with no progress made.

The situation lasted for more than three days before it settled down. But then, out of the blue, two prisoners died from the torture they'd suffered as a direct result of the uprising, after having been accused of inciting it. This was brutal. A general state of depression descended upon everyone. Bilal Salman and Ibrahim Abu al-Izz had been martyred and we no longer had news about many other prisoners. The two men's souls joined those of the other noble and honorable brothers who preceded them—Abdullah Hamza and Hajj Ahmad Termus, for example, who died as a result of torture and cold showers in the freezing cold of winter.

The incident deeply impacted everyone. It emboldened us beyond measure. The martyrdom of these two men gave rise to an unbreakable resolve in us, the ability to face any fate, whatever it may be. But what would their family's response be? What would they be told? They'd waited a long time for their return, but a lifeless body is no kind of return. Their memory, however, remains eternal, in the pulse of every male and female prisoner. This was true to the point that every time we would see a male prisoner, we always saw Bilal or Ibrahim in him. Despair will not control the souls of those left behind. The road is long.

Days and weeks rolled by and nothing new happened, except for a few small changes. We were allowed more access to prison officials, we saw tiny improvements in our living conditions, and we did obtain some releases. None of this would have even been possible had the blood of Bilal, Ibrahim, and others like them not been spilled.

## WINTER TRAGEDIES

Winter arrived. The bitter cold lashes into too-thin bodies and all you have to keep you warm are your clothes and two shabby blankets to wrap around your skinny frame. Water would leak into our cells from the windows, and very often our clothes and bedding would get so wet that the discomfort woke us up. We would try everything to prevent our clothes from getting soaked, but it was useless.

The switching of prisoners' cells continued for as long as our imprisonment did, so eventually, K.A. was transferred to our cell. She'd been arrested while carrying out a military operation with seven of her Palestinian resistance fighter brothers in the town of Kafr Kila.[29] She was only sixteen years old. By the time she was transferred to our cell, she'd been in prison for about two months. She told us the story of how she'd gotten arrested with her comrades. One of the people of the town of Kafr Kila ratted them out, even though someone had vouched for him. Now she's like any other prisoner. I learned many revolutionary songs from her. I also listened to her tell many heroic stories. We spent most of our time in prayer, doing exercise, and fasting on important religious occasions. One day we agreed to fast together. When it came time to break our fast, dinner consisted of a can of sardines and a boiled potato.

Shortly after we'd broken our fast, we felt thirsty. The weather outside was rainy, but there was nothing to drink. What could we do? We weren't allowed to fill up our water at this time of day, and we couldn't stand the thirst. We decided to knock on our cell door and ask the guard for some water. But this terrible woman refused, reprimanding us in the process. I started cursing and swearing, as did my cellmates. I went back to my spot in the corner of the cell, looking at my cellmates who were still cursing the state we'd found ourselves in. I contemplated them, looking at each one by one, listening to the sound of rain outside while in desperate need of a drop of water to drink. Then I turned my gaze toward the iron bars on the windows, focusing on the sound of the

---

29    The town of Kafr Kila is in the district of Marjayoun, about 31 kilometers from Bint Jbeil, MA and MH.

rain pattering against them.

A piece of cloth that we'd put over the window to prevent our things from getting wet caught my attention. Next to this piece of cloth there were several dried onions that had been distributed with breakfast. A drop of water dripped quickly off the cloth. It occurred to me that I could put a box that was originally used for sweets underneath it and collect the rainwater. I did this without anyone noticing. I waited for a good amount of time until the container was half full and then I emptied it into the plastic jug. Then I pretended to check for any water in any container in the cell and acted surprised that I had just suddenly found this water in the jug. I told K.A. to drink from it, but she refused and insisted that I drink first. Because of her insistence, I drank a little. I'll never forget that terrible taste! Then I passed the jug to her and as soon as she sipped the water she yelped, "What did I just drink?"

This ruckus caused the guard to come and pound on our door, asking what was going on. We replied, "Nothing." K.A. started squeaking, asking me what she'd drunk. With a smile and ice running through my veins I replied, "Haven't you heard of the proverb that says, 'I have drunk bitterness'? We drink all kinds of bitterness here in prison. What we just drank is onion juice." The incident somewhat alleviated the gloomy atmosphere in the cell, and the girls in the cell next door rushed to the window to ask us about the screaming. K.A. told them what had happened, and they erupted in laughter. We could hear it through the window. This was one of the many incidents that was precipitated by our difficult living conditions.

Days inched on, as slow as a tortoise. Then May 17, 1989 arrived. This date is now known by everyone, because it is the anniversary of the 17 May Agreement with the Israelis—but this agreement for normalization and surrender collapsed thanks to national political resolve. On this Wednesday in May, G.A. was moved into my cell. This rarely happened—putting two prisoners from the same town, involved in the same operation, in a cell together. It was a wonderful thing for me, for her, and for the women prisoners. We had a warm reunion, and from the second we saw each other, the questions we had for each other practically spilled out of us. "Since you were arrested three days after me, do you know what happened to my siblings?" I asked her.

"I didn't see any of your siblings, but I knew of your arrest when it happened. The news shocked everyone. No one could believe that you had anything to do with this operation. You surprised us all. No one saw this coming."

I replied, "That's the most important thing. When we carry out these operations, we can't let our oppressive enemy notice that anything is out of order. Otherwise, how can we succeed? Anyway, what was the reason they gave for your arrest?"

"That disturbed woman ratted me out," she said. She meant F.Y. "The worst part is that I didn't actually do anything for this operation. But I do remember her asking me to record the names of the guards they read out over the loudspeakers at the mosque. I didn't know why she asked me to do that at the time."

I replied, "The reason doesn't matter now, what matters is that it seems they will release you soon, otherwise they wouldn't have put you in the same cell with me. Let's hope it's true!"

I spent a month or more in a cell with her, and we talked constantly about our families and our town. One day, after I came back from the shower, I found her slowly pacing up and down the cell. We had another discussion about our families then, and because they were likely to release her before me, I started counselling her on what she could say to my family in the event that she did get out. She did the same with me, in case I was released first. Sure enough, my intuition had not lied. While we were talking, the guard came to our cell and opened the door unexpectedly. She told G.A. to collect her things and her mattress and to follow her. Without thinking, I exclaimed, "Liberation!" The guard answered, "Who told you that? We're only transferring her to another cell." I truly believed that G.A. was going to be released. After she'd left the cell, my cellmates could see movement outside. We waited for about a quarter of an hour, but no other door was opened. G.A. had indeed been released!

We were all filled with joy, and through the windows we all offered each other wishes that the other would be next. Each of us wished the other freedom from prison as soon as possible.

Then the days went back to their boring, monotonous rhythm. Often we killed time by creating our handicrafts, concealing this from the guards. Our diverse artwork expressed many things; our crafts were all touched by the spirit of resistance. For example, we depicted a resistance fighter carrying a rifle and scaling barbed wire, near the family tree that every prisoner had contributed to.

Prisoners started getting shuffled around cells again. A new prisoner was brought to our cell from the village of Blat.[30] She had been in prison for about a month at the time.

Her interrogations were over, and as usual we heaped many questions upon her. One person asked her about the security situation outside the prison, another about her village—perhaps she'd heard some news about it. Yet another person asked her about the economic situation, or if she'd heard anything about any plans for prisoner releases. She answered all of these questions offhandedly; it seemed as if these things no longer concerned her. But they were very important to us. She appeared to be strong-willed and not interested in anything to do with the prison. She said at the very beginning, "No matter how long we're in prison, we will be released one day." The way she spoke was reassuring. She spent a long time with us, contemplating her release, however long it would take. Though at times she was filled with despair, she always appeared indifferent no matter what was going on.

## AN OPERATION ON MY FEET INSIDE PRISON

I started to feel a slight pain in my feet, as a result of being severely beaten with a whip during a torture session. After this, my health started

---

30  The village of Blat is in the Marjayoun district, about 44 kilometers from Bint Jbeil. MA and MH.

deteriorating until, at my fifteenth hospital visit, I was told I weighed only thirty-nine kilograms. I'd been there many times because of complications due to the two-year interruption to my menstrual cycle. The doctor asked how much I'd weighed when they'd first detained me. At that time, I'd weighed about fifty-five kilos.

As the days passed, the pain in my feet grew worse until I was no longer able to walk normally. I repeatedly insisted on seeing the doctor to find out the cause of my pain, but to no avail—they just gave me painkillers. It got worse until I could no longer sleep or walk properly. The painkillers turned into sleeping pills, but nothing worked. My cellmates even started to agonize with me, as they weren't able to sleep through the night because of my constant shrieks of pain. One night, my cellmate, S.E., started banging on the cell door violently, paying no heed to any potential punishment, shouting at the top of her lungs, "She's going to die from this pain, what's wrong with you? Why aren't you doing anything?"

In response, they put her in solitary confinement for two days. We went on hunger strike and I begged for her to be returned to the cell because she didn't deserve that punishment. It was only because of me that she was put in solitary. I asked to go in her place. They returned her to the cell after we threatened to continue our hunger strike. All the guards did for me was call the nurse, who summoned me and started experimenting on me in the guard's room. He inserted a syringe into my feet, and it filled with pus, which was a clear sign of severe cyanosis. Without using any disinfectant, he stuck the needle back into my feet several times to see what would happen next. This experiment made things worse. Afterwards the nurse ordered me to go back to my cell, promising to take me to hospital the next day. When evening fell, my feet had swelled up even more and severe pains were shooting through my body. I didn't sleep a wink that night, and neither did anyone else in the cell as they tried to do whatever they could to help relieve my pain. My friend F.R. put cool compresses on my feet continually and stayed awake with me all night. S.E. stroked my head gently, hoping to help me doze off a little.

I felt the strongest and most sincere sisterly love from them, standing in for the love and tenderness of my own family. They were truly sisters in every meaning of the word, sisters who stayed with me when my screaming grew louder. I shouted out all kinds of words that I was not even aware of, but which my friends told me about later: "I've never felt such pain in my entire life. If I divided this pain among all of us in prison, there would be enough to go around and then some!" I don't know how the sun rose the next day. As soon as the guard opened the door, my friends began to protest that I'd been neglected, and the guards promised to inform the warden about what had happened. They said that perhaps I'd be moved to the hospital that day.

But I wasn't satisfied with his promise and made an official request to the guards to inform the warden that I wanted to meet him in person. But he didn't respond to my request. At around 9:30 AM, the guards told me to get myself ready because I was being transferred to hospital. And indeed a few hours later the guard came back with handcuffs and a bag to put over my head. I thought I was alone in the ambulance, but there was a male prisoner with me in the vehicle. I was eager to find out who he was, and I tried to speak to him. It was an indescribable surprise for me to learn that this prisoner was from my same town and was in fact R.D.—one of our neighbor's sons who'd been arrested about a year and a half before I was.

And it appeared that even he was not alone. There was another male prisoner with us as well. I asked him how he was doing with great difficulty, as I had to keep this concealed from the guard, and I learned that he was suffering from severe stomach pains. The guard realized what was going on between us and she and the nurse both threatened us to remain silent for the rest of the trip. But I was curious to know who the other prisoner was. He was from the town of Maroun al-Ras,[31] and he suffered from ear pain so bad that he couldn't hear well. That's what R.D. told me in the ambulance. When we arrived at the hospital, we

---

31  Maroun al-Ras is located in the Bint Jbeil district and is only about 4 kilometers from the town of Bint Jbeil. MA and MH.

were separated. They put me in a room, the guard slowly leading the way. Perhaps she was waiting for people to move away from the area we were passing through. I heard a voice telling the guard to take the bag off my head and release my handcuffs. She did so. I looked around. It was the first time I'd seen a person from the world of freedom. Lying on the table as the doctor had asked me to, I started looking all around the room.

He asked me what was wrong, and I told him. He then began examining my feet. He was shocked at the sight of them and asked the guard, "Why didn't you bring her in sooner? The state of her feet is so bad that she needs emergency surgery, right this second." The guard summoned the nurse. He might have been the one escorting the male prisoners. There was also a guard whose pseudonym was Abdullah. She informed him that the doctor was going to perform emergency surgery. The nurse replied, "He can't do it right now because we have to get permission from the warden first." The doctor replied, "Her situation is intolerable. But if this is how things are, then bring her back first thing tomorrow morning." They took me back to prison with the others. Everyone was waiting. "Can you believe that they didn't do my surgery because they need official permission from the warden? Even if we're on the verge of death, they'll do nothing without permission. They're killing us. This is unlivable." I kept repeating this, banging against the iron door, until the guard came to open it and ask what was going on. My friends protested what was happening to me, saying that my situation could not be borne any longer, and that my surgery shouldn't be delayed.

I swore and I cursed, and the guard's response was to ask the nurse to give me enough painkillers to see me through until morning. But what pills could even scratch the surface of the pain I was in? The next day came and then the next and still I wasn't taken to hospital. My condition worsened and I was in constant pain, at the outer limits of what a human can endure. You could clearly see the pus filling my feet. Three days later I was sent to hospital and I had the surgery. I didn't know how much time I spent there, but I do remember the doctor's astonishment at how much he drained from my feet, as well as his surprise at my ability to endure such extreme pain. They took me back to prison after wrapping my feet in bandages. The doctor asked them to bring me back each day to change the dressings.

Back in our cell, my sister-cellmates gathered around me, and all the other sister-prisoners checked in on how I was doing. After some time had passed, the pain returned. I couldn't move or even speak. Two things flashed through my mind that day: an image I'd seen in the ambulance when I was going to hospital and what I'd heard the nurse say about one of the prisoners. I will never forget what I saw on the way to hospital that day. I was able to lift the bag off my face a little, and I could see one of the prisoners lying on a stretcher in the vehicle. My eyes were drawn to his hands which had clear signs of torture on them—I could tell that they had put out cigarette butts on them. The sounds of his moaning interrupted the silence from time to time.

Inside the hospital, I heard the nurse speaking to the doctor and asking him to perform surgery on the prisoner. I heard the doctor telling him that surgery was not necessary. The nurse replied, "Do the operation so I don't have to keep hearing his voice, Doc. Every few minutes his friends call out to me, 'Nurse, he's too worn out, he can't stand the pain any longer.'" Curses on those jailers and a thousand more on the interrogators who have led people to this stage. Thinking of this moment made me forget my pain a little; my soul was comforted by this thought. I kept telling my friends what I'd seen and heard, and you could see its impact on their faces. One of them even started crying. We are all sisters and brothers in tragedy and torment.

The day after the operation, I asked for my bandages to be changed and said that I needed anti-inflammatory medications. But this only happened two days later. The same scenario repeated itself not long after, and nothing happened. Instead, my cellmates and I cleaned the wound with water and wrapped my feet in a piece of cloth. But my feet soon became sore and irritated once again and their condition kept deteriorating. I still regularly feel the pain in my feet today, despite the years that have passed.

Our monotonous, deadly routine resumed. One day, a friend suggested that I ask the prison warden to be allowed to have the books for my university studies brought to me in prison. I did so, but he refused sarcastically, "You're asking the impossible. We didn't bring you here so you could study and become educated. And in any case, this would be up to the Israelis, not me."

I never lost sight of the fact that the enemy was fighting against us even at the level of our education. They wished to prevent us from learning. But their attempts were futile. We found solace in our conversations; talking through the windows had a particular way of fortifying us because it was considered a challenge to their authority. My friend K.Z. was in Cell Three and I was still in Cell Five, as the two of us especially were not allowed to be in one cell. K.Z. told me that she would ask the warden for permission to see me in the guards' room to check up on my health after my surgery. I laughed sarcastically at that. Would they allow it? To see her specifically? But she was indeed allowed to. Our reunion was joyful but mixed with pain and bitterness. It lasted for only five minutes and we were in the constant presence of guards who hovered near us to prevent the exchange of any conversation or words about anything other than good wishes for my health and recovery. A few weeks later, K.Z. asked to see F.Y., and she was allowed to do that too, after some insistence.

I wish that had never happened. When K.Z. met F.Y. and hugged her, she whispered in her ear to stop collaborating with them. This is what K.Z. reported to us when she was back in the cell after their meeting. It didn't even take a half hour for K.Z. to be put into solitary confinement after that. The reason was clear to everyone. F.Y. had informed on K.Z. and told the guard what she'd said. And as a result, K.Z. had been put in the Hole. We all protested and demanded she be returned to her cell, but that only happened a week later.

This is the kind of thing that inside informers did.

## A FRANK CONFESSION

About two and a half years after my arrest, F.Y. asked the prison warden to be transferred into my cell. She got what she wanted, of course. How could it be otherwise, when she functioned as the eyes and ears of the interrogators, the warden, and the guards inside and outside of our cells? I couldn't imagine being stuck in a cell with her, or her sharing one with any of the rest of the brave women militants for that matter. How awful! They all looked at her with contempt and disgust. Why did she do this? Why does she collaborate with them? And why is she with us now? We all asked ourselves many questions about her and dealt with her cautiously. I felt I was constantly on the verge of losing my temper. Isn't what she did to us enough? Why is she here with us now? But my fellow prisoners tried to keep me calm and asked me not to jump the gun. I thought I could pretend to act calm and friendly towards her. Perhaps then I could get her to confess to collaborating with them and thus find out why she'd done it. Maybe I could also find out what had happened to her from the time of her arrest until now. Surely, she knows everything that's going on. She and others like her are allowed to see their families and she must know all about what is going on in the outside world.

A few days later, I felt that I had taken on a difficult task, and if I didn't accomplish it something bad would happen. I didn't know what that would be, but it was important to me that she confess what she'd done. What I was hoping for came true. I started talking to her and making it clear that we all knew about her collaboration with the enemy—hers and other people's too.

She started telling me her story, how she'd started collaborating from the time of her arrest, and that she did this as a result of the huge pressure they were putting on her. They'd threatened to kill members of her family, destroy her family's house, and made all kinds of other threats that interrogators always make with both male and female prisoners. Her justifications for her collaboration were not reason enough for her to do this and I made this clear to her. I told her that we'd all been subjected to the pressure of the same threats. What she and those like her had done betrayed a weakness of will; they sold their souls out for cheap.

After she confessed all of this to me, narrating and talking about it as if it were the most natural thing in the world, she then also told me how she'd met with a security official from Lahad's Army in Bint Jbeil inside the prison and how he solicited her to collaborate with them. This was also normal for her, because the filth of who you mix with rubs off on you, and you become as filthy as they are in the process. She went on to admit to me that the collaborating security agent from my town, Fawzi al-Saghir, was there when she agreed to become an informer, and that he'd encouraged her to do so. She began in early June, a month and a few days after her arrest and imprisonment.

She told me which men and women from our town were there and who among these people had been arrested and detained for hours, without anyone knowing a thing about their whereabouts—some people for days and others for weeks. She even admitted to me that her family had visited her from time to time and shared news with her. She reassured me that my family and the families of everyone in prison were all fine. She informed me of all of this as if it were an important achievement of hers. She concluded her confession by repenting what she had done. But what kind of repentance was it?

I could no longer tolerate sharing a cell with her. I told my friends what she'd confessed to me. Though we already knew what she'd done, her admission had a painful effect on our souls, despite the repentance she'd declared.

Her behavior in the cell negated this repentance. When we would hear the voice of one of the prisoners screaming out in pain while being tortured, she would pace back and forth in the cell, saying to herself aloud, "Why doesn't he confess? Isn't that better than torture? He's getting what he deserves, why doesn't he just confess?"

It was as if she didn't realize who she was with, there in that cell. Her heart had hardened like theirs. Her behavior made her presence in our cell more and more intolerable until I burst out yelling, "Get her out of here, she's a liar and a fraud! Isn't what she's already done to us enough?" The other prisoners started to try to assuage my anger, though they felt no less anger and resentment than I did. Eventually she herself asked to be removed from the cell and went back to collaborating with them. Whenever she heard a conversation between prisoners through the window, she would rush to inform the guards so that those she'd informed on would be punished. After all of this, is it possible to forgive the traitors who are more dangerous to the prisoners than even the interrogators and torturers themselves?

## A DREAM I WILL NEVER FORGET

I'd been in prison for about two years when I had a dream I'll never forget. I had this dream in addition to the other typical dreams that every prisoner experiences—about being freed from prison or being rearrested and sent back. But this specific dream recurred regularly for the rest of the time I was in prison. I dreamed that my brother had been shot in our town, and that he had died as a result. I woke up from my deep sleep in terror, screaming at the top of my lungs. My shouts woke all the other prisoners, and the guards came and banged on the door to find out the reason for all the screaming. One of my cellmates replied that I was just having a nightmare. This was at about two o'clock in the morning. I continued to have that recurring dream many nights afterwards. The tragedy came upon my release. Ten days after I was freed, I was shocked to learn that the brother I'd dreamed about had indeed been martyred. His death coincided with the exact time at which I'd had the dream, which I still cannot forget, to this day. It happened on July, 15 1990.

The routine switching around of prisoners continued. This time, Soha Bechara was transferred to a new building in the prison. They put her in Cell Twenty-Four, facing the cell I was in at the time. Our cell looked directly out onto that one. When night fell, I climbed up on a barrel which doubled as a toilet and opened the window to be able to peer out. I kept making sounds, which were a secret code, so that we could talk to each other.

Soha also climbed up to the window of her cell and we talked for what felt like forever. She told me about the most important political events and operations against the military, as well as their impact on the prisoners. She also talked about prison conditions. She said that I might be in prison for considerably longer than others, as my assassination attempt was not all that different from hers, except that she was able to carry hers out while mine was aborted before it could be put into motion.

There we were, waiting for nightfall and for the guards to turn in so that we could discuss issues related to prisoners and our conditions inside the prison. One day, Soha was taken to the warden's office. I wondered what was going on; we all did, and we were waiting for her to return. When we finally had the opportunity to talk, she told us that she'd requested a meeting with the Israelis to present the prisoners' demands. The most important of these was improving the way we were treated, allowing us materials for handicrafts, and books to read. They responded that they would study these matters, but the more time passed the clearer it became that they would not meet our demands. The only thing that they allowed us to do during this period was play cards. Even though I didn't enjoy playing cards, we were able to make things out of them that we couldn't before. We managed to fashion a bag to hold our clothes out of bits of blanket and blue jeans, for example. If it hadn't been for all those restrictions, and if they hadn't rejected every one of our demands, preventing us from living our lives in a way that helped us overcome the bitterness of time and the deadliness of boredom, things would have been different.

It was very common for serious health problems to run rampant through the female prison population, and the same was true for the male prisoners. Sounds of people screaming in pain rang in our ears constantly. One of them kept imploring the guard to call the nurse, but no one paid him any mind. None of their hearts had even a trace of humanity left in them. After you call out for a long time, a loud voice orders you to be quiet, to be completely silent. They just want a break from hearing your groaning, imploring them, "Nurse… please, guard, bring the nurse, I can't take the pain!"

Soon you go back to your spot in your cell and everyone whose turn will soon come gathers around you, signs of illness visible on their faces as well. Much of this is due to the polluted drinking water, lethal humidity levels, poor ventilation which prevents people from breathing properly, insufficient nutrition, and the lack of food. All of this will inevitably lead to the spread of disease, or even to epidemics. You go back to your spot. Your prison sisters rally around you, offering comfort and curses. One of them swears and explodes into tears. The same situation is repeated in one cell after the other, among the men and women alike.

Skin diseases afflict some of us, but there is no sufficient care available. This kind of condition can worsen to the point of the dry skin bleeding from constant scratching, or from rubbing it against the wall. It makes you long for death to spare you such pain.

Soha and all of the rest of the female prisoners protested against the situation K.Z. and K.A. were in. We made continual demands that they be treated and provided with at least the minimum standards of health care and hygiene. But the result was nothing but a bit of disinfectant and some first aid supplies like oxygen and iodine. This was not enough to treat the serious skin condition that had spread over their entire bodies. Both K.Z. and K.A. were isolated and put in solitary confinement as their condition continued to worsen. They insisted on seeing a specialist doctor at their own expense. But this wasn't within the realm of possibility for those of us subjected to the cruelty of prison rules.

You weren't arrested and imprisoned to be offered decent medical care. You have to try and maintain the bare minimum of your will to live—so you have something to fall back on when you're finally released. The prisoner Ahmad Bazzi from Bint Jbeil failed to hold onto even this most minimal will to survive, after being held in prison for five years. His health continued to deteriorate, and he received no treatment. Similarly, the prisoner Haytham Dabaja, also from Bint Jbeil, had been detained for ten years. Haytham began suffering from severe chest pains. He suffered and suffered and was treated in hospital, then was discharged back to prison, "It's nothing... just nerves. When you're released, it will get better. Take these pills and get some rest." He's now resting eternally; his life departed his body, just as so many others' lives had. They died in the cells they'd long dreamed of leaving. Yes, he did leave, but he departed for the afterlife.

There's no longer the need for a nurse or anyone else now that he's in his permanent resting place. What heartache for the family! To be returned after such a long wait, and what a return that is... It's all so cursed: iron bars, the whip, and interrogators... all of them come together to act out this brutal play of death. Just you wait, there are many more who are threatened with this sort of slumber—perhaps it will be temporary, but then again, it may last forever.

"We refuse to die! Tell them we are staying,"[32] we would repeat, lumps straining our throats. But we carried on. We female prisoners experienced the loss of a number of honorable heroes as well. Their souls permeated every corner of the prison. They whisper to everyone that they aren't dead. The road is long, and the journey continues.

Our communication with our fellow prisoners on the men's side in Prison Four was cut off with the construction of the new Women's Prison. All that reached us was the sound of cell doors opening and intermittent chatter when people spoke in very loud voices. Soha became the means of communication between us and the people behind the wall of her cell, which abutted theirs. If a day went by without any news from the men, Soha would signal to find out the reason why. Fairouz was there, as Soha sang her song, "Where are they, where oh where are they? There's a valley now between me and them..."[33] She would wait for a bit, and if there was no response, she would sing again. Their voices would then reply in song

---

32　These are lyrics from the Julia Boutros song, "Ghabet Shams El Haqq."

33　The famous song by the Lebanese diva Fairouz was sung in the play "The Guardian of the Keys {Natouret al-Mafatih}," arranged by the Rahbani brothers in 1972.

and Soha's laughter would ring out to let us know that they were fine and that there was nothing to worry about.

We would wait for nightfall so we could speak face-to-face. In our discussions, I asked if she expected any kind of release to come soon. She answered, "I do expect there to be a release soon, but I am ruling you and me out from that. Our cases are similar—the only difference is that I was able to go further in my operation than you were because you were arrested too soon." She continued, "I do however expect that they will release K.Z. because of her skin disease." We carried on talking for hours without feeling the time pass. We talked like that the entire time that Soha was in the cell across from ours.

On Wednesday, September 9, 1991, at approximately two in the afternoon, the first large batch of prisoners was released. They let out fifty-one prisoners, alive and martyred, including five young women. This restored hope to many people who had convinced themselves that they'd been born and would die here. Indeed, I was one of those who had resigned myself to this fate.

Exactly forty days after this batch was released, in the month of October, they released another group of thirteen prisoners including one of ours—K.Z. Her chance to meet her loved ones had arrived. But it's sad for a person to be released when other loved ones, prison sisters and brothers, remain in this cemetery. What is the meaning of this long-awaited freedom with others still inside? The joy of freedom and liberation cannot truly be experienced until everyone inside is released. All of us shared this powerful feeling: every single one of us hoped for the other women's release before our own.

It was the first of December of the same year, 1991, on a Sunday at about 9 o'clock in the morning—a routine day, like any other. We were getting ready for our scheduled shower. On that particular day, we had no hope of being released since it was a public holiday: on holidays, there isn't usually much going on inside the prison, except the kinds of things that never take a break, day or night, things that don't take even one day off. The guard opened the door to announce that it was shower time and told me to come with her. I thought that she was asking me to do that day's kilfa, cleaning the interrogation room. But instead she took me into the guards' room. When I was there, she told me that I should get myself ready and collect my belongings. I asked her why. She smiled and I felt that something was up, something more than a cell trade.

"Don't you dare tell anyone, but you are being released soon." I didn't believe what I'd just heard, and I wanted to cry. Why, I don't know, but I thought that she was trying to play with my emotions. My face grew dark. The guard noticed this, and repeated herself, "I'm telling you the truth, the warden asked us to inform you. It's you and another girl called Rabab." Rabab is from the town of Khiam and was in prison with her sister, who'd shared a cell with me for about a year and a half. I couldn't believe it despite her insistence that it was true. I wanted to go back to my cell immediately as my feet could no longer hold me upright. A few minutes later, they took me back to my cell so I could get ready, making me promise not to tell anyone.

As soon as she closed the door on me, I rushed to my sister prisoners to kiss them and tell them about what had happened. Then I climbed up to the window to tell everyone else about this as well. It brought great joy to everyone, especially I.A. who was with me in the cell, because her sister was going to be released. I couldn't hold back my tears, and neither could my friends. My joy at being free was immense, but my grief for those I would leave behind was greater. I wished so much that they could be released before me. I climbed up to the window across from Soha's cell and started sending out code words as a signal for her to climb up and talk to me. As soon as she was up there, she sent me blessings on my freedom, before I'd even told her my news. She'd figured out what was happening from movements in front of her cell and the guards' room. She was always closely observing everything going on. She was very happy about this, and she told me that my deteriorating health and psychological state had helped me gain my release. Oh, how I wished that they all would have been released before me.

It is the wish of every male and female prisoner—to see everyone else freed first!

The guard returned to take me from the cell. I started hugging and kissing everyone. It's a difficult moment because it's like leaving a part of yourself behind. You are leaving one family to reunite with another. It is one of the strangest and most difficult emotions a person can experience. I was taken to the warden's office and I found my friend Rabab there. I was very happy to see several of my brother prisoners standing in front of vehicles belonging to the International Red Cross. I felt like I was seeing brothers of mine after a long absence, though I didn't even know their names. Inside, the warden asked me to stand against the wall where one of them took two pictures of me—one straight on and one of my profile.

There were a number of people in the room, including someone working for the International Red Cross. I could tell this from the badge on his clothes. He was seated next to the prison nurse, the security official, a number of the interrogators, and the male guards.

The warden asked me to approach his desk and started saying, "Today you are being released. But if you commit any acts of sabotage, no matter how minor, you will be returned here and stay forever. You must sign here to state that you agree to these conditions."

After signing the document, which was as useless as they were, the Red Cross representative asked me about my health and my weight before my arrest. A little while later, this person drove me to the Red Cross vehicle with a number of guards. There were one hundred and twenty-five prisoners there, including two female prisoners—me and my friend Rabab. We were the second batch being released as part of a prisoner exchange, for two people being held—one of which was Terry Waite, the other Terry Anderson. There were three of us from the same town. One of us was called Ghassan Beydoun. He had been in a painful accident in the prison kitchen and lost his hearing in one ear when a pot of boiling water spilled on him and burned him. He'd spent a full month in the hospital, being taken back and forth to prison, but to no avail. I was happy for him, as were all of the prisoners. We set off in two cars, with a jeep belonging to the Lahad militia in front of us, and another behind us.

Just a few meters after passing through the prison gates, we were greeted by a chicken near the side of the road. Someone shouted out, "Hey, check it out, chickens still look the same!" We exploded in laughter.

I don't know why, but I felt that there was still something in store for me. My heart was pounding against my ribcage as we arrived at the Marjayoun barracks. This is where they separated those who would be released to regions outside of the occupied zone from those who would be allowed to remain. I was among the latter, as were five others, including my friend. From there, we were transferred to Bint Jbeil with the other male prisoner from our town, in a car belonging to the Lebanese Red Cross. I didn't know what was happening around me and I didn't understand this scattering of people. The car set off and as we got closer to our destination, my heart started squeezing and contracting. I don't know why, but I was quiet most of the way. As soon as we entered town, a civilian car with three women, driven by a man, pulled up next to us. They waved their hands and signaled us to stop. They got out of the car. I was taken aback. "Who are these people?" I wondered. Our car stopped alongside theirs. It turned out to be the family of the male prisoner who was with us, whom I did not know and had never seen in town before. They asked the driver of the Red Cross vehicle to let their son ride with them in their car. But he refused saying that we had to be dropped off at our homes and that's where they could sign for him. We then continued our journey until we reached this man's house. He was then handed over to his family who'd all gathered there. Then the car continued on, towards my house, which I guided the driver to.

By the time I arrived home, a crowd of people had already gathered there waiting for me, none of whom I even recognized. They told me that everyone in my family was fine and that my sister would soon catch me up on everything. But where was my sister? She screamed my name at the top of her lungs the moment she saw me, through her tears. I don't know how to articulate the feeling that washed over me, it was indescribable.

I clasped her eagerly and powerfully, holding onto her. I didn't want to relax our embrace for even one second. I saw every member of my family in her. We went into the house with all these people crowding around me. I didn't understand what was going on. I couldn't even process where I was. I sat down and made my sister sit down right next to me; I kept hugging her close. Some of the people around also came in, others left congratulating me on my freedom and my safe return home.

I felt trapped in a vortex. But despite this, I alternated between greeting everyone who had come to welcome me back home and asking my sister about our family. She kept reassuring me that everyone was fine, "Some of our cousins have babies, and even more than one, since you've been in prison. I'll show you pictures this evening." Despite her assurances, I could still feel my heart pinching tight and I wanted to leave and go see the rest of my family.

But I would need an official pass for that. How could I get one? How could I go to the permit center in person? The third day after my release, I went to the center they told me about, but there were so many people there—none of whom I knew—and I couldn't get a pass. I had to return the following day. The same thing happened again. The stalling process had begun. I was referred from one person to another, all of whom were collaborators. An employee there advised me to put it off until the next day. They later informed me that permits had to be obtained directly from the collaborating agent, Husayn Abdel-Nabi, Enemy-Nabi. What irony! He was still alive?

My first thought was: "His day is coming soon, God willing." I returned to my family's house only to be surprised by a Lebanese Red Cross vehicle that was there asking about me. They had been contacted by my family who'd started to have doubts I'd actually been released, despite hearing my name in the media. I explained to them what was going on.

I told the Red Cross worker what was happening to me—that the agents were refusing to issue me a travel permit. He replied that they would follow up on it themselves. And on the ninth day after my release, a person came to me and said that Abdel-Nabi wanted to meet me at the permit center. That person escorted me to a meeting with Abdel-Nabi on December 17. I never thought that I would see his cursed face ever again.

As soon as we arrived, Abdel-Nabi began twirling and swirling his words—which I neither cared to hear nor understand. All that mattered was that I get the permit. He kept stalling but I eventually got what I wanted: a permit. Though he made sure I knew that he could invalidate it any time he wanted. As soon as I got it and left the center, I rushed to my sister's house. The moment I arrived, I informed her that I'd gotten the permit and that I had to leave town the next day. I would have left then and there but it was too late in the day.

The next day, Wednesday December 18, 1991, was the true day of my release. I left my town and never looked back. I crossed the checkpoint not believing that I was now out of the grip of those bastards. I reached the town where my family was living, and the moment of our reunion is one I will never forget. Everyone crowded around me, but I knew who each one was this time! My youngest brother who was only eleven years old when I was arrested was now a young man. He came over to hug me, but startled, I pushed him back and asked, "Who are you?" I didn't recognize him at first. "I'm your brother!" That was difficult to process. I started checking through everyone—"Where is my brother Jamal?" I didn't see him or his wife and son—surely his son was old enough to be there. When I'd left, the baby was a year and a half old, and while I was in prison, he'd also had a daughter who was already two. "Where are they? I want to see them!"

"He's away, his family is coming over soon. He'll be so happy to hear the news of your release."

Their answers to my questions about my brother made me suspicious, especially since they said that he was "away"—I knew he always refused to travel, no matter what. I felt there was something off, and I didn't believe this story about him travelling, nor what they'd told me about him.

I sat there just staring at everyone, taking them all in. I hugged them, kissed them, and stroked their faces. How much they had all changed!

I was surprised at the state of my father, who was very thin. Where had his strong body gone? He had suffered from a serious health scare as a result of my arrest—he'd had a stroke—but he'd made a miraculous recovery.

"Mom, why are there tears in your eyes?"

"I'm just so happy to see you, my sweet daughter."

I hugged and kissed her, wiped away her tears and asked her to smile from now on, because the torment had passed. "I'm here with you now, and I'm in great shape." But she wouldn't stop crying. I intuited that she was only pretending that these were tears of joy. I had a sneaking suspicion that her continuous weeping, which lasted a full twenty days after my release, was also lamenting the news of my brother's martyrdom.

It was as if I already knew this on some level, because I'd seen in it my dream. I realized that the real reason for the tightness in my chest and the pinching at my heart was that I had a date with misery. I spent the first night back with my family in my mother's arms. She kept crying and then would suddenly stop and ask me about my health, and what had happened to me in there. I didn't tell her anything too specific about life in prison: "The important thing is that I'm back and here with you now. But please, mom, pray with me. Ask God to release everyone else. My heart and mind are there with them still."

She prayed out loud, "God, please unite every mother with her child, as You have returned mine to me." Her sobs were not far behind. It was a night washed in tears. Tears of joy mixed with tears of sadness, whose secret I only unlocked later. As the days passed, I found myself in a society unfamiliar to me. Or perhaps I was unfamiliar to it—it was as if I'd been cut off from the world for dozens of years.

Everything had changed. The news of my brother's martyrdom affected me for a long time—not because he had been martyred; I am proud of him for doing that. It was for one reason alone: I had been so excited to see him. We were so close, it felt like we were twins. I was cloaked in sadness and found it difficult to enjoy my freedom. And every morning I woke, every moment that passed, reminded me of the brother and sister prisoners I'd left behind. I wondered what they were doing.

Soon after, I also had to mourn the passing of my mother. The meaning of life changed for me. This is how fate works: nothing befalls us except what God has decreed for us (Q 9:52). I had to follow my faith and what I believed in. It was my duty after being released to do all I could to amplify the issue of prisoners and spread the word. No one knows the suffering of prisoners better than the prisoners themselves. And no prisoner can truly know the meaning of freedom until all prisons and all other kinds of detention centers are closed. Being imprisoned is a journey—for me it lasted much longer than just those four years. It is a decades-long, even centuries-long, journey, rife with all kinds of pain and torment. No matter how great a sacrifice a free person offers the homeland, it is never enough. They are propelled by their faith in God and country, as well as a personal impulse that can only accept to live a life of freedom and dignity.

I returned to a life of freedom. I am completely determined and hopeful that I can continue what I started—my own educational pursuits and activism for our country. I returned to my university studies after my release and am pursuing them with success. I will realize my hopes and ambitions. I am determined. All thanks to God, King of the Universe.

## EPILOGUE

After being released from prison, I resumed my university studies at the Faculty of Law in Saida. When I completed my degree, I worked as a teacher outside of the "border strip," or the security belt, as they called that area at the time. I had to live outside of Bint Jbeil because after my release from prison, I was expelled from the area and couldn't return until after the liberation of the South in the year 2000. But my activism did not stop after the liberation of the South. I carried on fighting for prisoners and detainees by helping establish the Lebanese Association for Prisoners and Liberators (LAPL).

One of the most important events I participated in after my release was a trip to Italy as part of a delegation that included a number of former prisoners. We took our case to the Pope in Rome. We also raised the issue at the international level through a number of sit-ins, as well as by submitting a note of protest to UN Secretary General, Kofi Annan, protesting the continued incarceration of many Lebanese prisoners inside occupied Palestine. After I'd been released from Khiam in a prisoner exchange, my main goal was to pursue the cause of all prisoners and detainees until we achieved complete liberation. Thanks to the resistance fighters who defeated the Zionist enemy, all remaining prisoners in Lebanon were liberated by the resistance and the people's struggle on May 23, 2000.

The most important thing that happened after I was released from prison was the assassination of that damned Israeli collaborator agent Husayn Abdel-Nabi. It was an unforgettable day. I'd been free for almost a year when he was killed.

It was a weekday morning. As soon as I got to the school where I was teaching at the time, the headmaster approached me with a smile on his face. I couldn't read through it. He said to me, "We want the reward for this good news!"

"What good news?"

"Husayn Abdel-Nabi has been assassinated."

Though I had been expecting our resistance fighters to do this at any moment, when the day actually came it was like nothing I had experienced in my entire lifetime. I rushed out to buy sweets and started passing them out to members of the teaching staff. I'll never forget how it felt to receive this news.

I finally went back to Bint Jbeil after the liberation of the South. I now work as a hall monitor in the Bint Jbeil Secondary School. My prison story is not so different from those of other prisoners. I wrote it down and published it so that these memories could be preserved over time, and so that in times of peace we will never forget our struggles living under occupation.

We are powerful and victorious because of the blood spilled by our martyrs and the suffering of prisoners in detention. From behind bars, we have rewritten history and left our mark on it.

Those who have no history, have no future. History is victory, liberation, and freedom.

Nawal Baidoun during the visit to the Vatican to meet the Pope

Nawal Baidoun with Soha Bechara

# — TRANSLATORS' NOTE —

Moving Nawal Baidoun's story of her years in the Khiam Prison in South Lebanon into English was a project as inspiring as it was challenging. We worked together to translate the *Memoirs of a Militant: My Years in the Khiam Women's Prison* during the long COVID summer of 2020, in Montreal, talking and debating over email, WhatsApp, and Zoom, and at times managing to sit at a distance from each other outside. The collaborative part of this translation, we hope, has only made it better— a read as compelling in English as it is in Arabic. The story Nawal Baidoun tells here is raw—she wrote it shortly after being released from prison—and it offers the reader insight into so many things, starting from life under Israeli occupation, passing through the lives led under the incredibly cruel conditions of the Khiam Prison, and culminating in Baidoun's release from what she called "the graveyard." Throughout all this runs a constant thread of resistance to oppression and survival in the face of hardship. Importantly, it ends with the call for the abolition of prisons in all their forms, something that still resonates strongly today.

All works present challenges when being shifted into another language—some are similar to each other and some are unique. Here we wish to draw out some of the specific translation issues we met in translating this Arabic text into English and give some explanations of the way we responded to them. We do this to offer the reader insights into the original text as well as to shine a light on the very different contexts that Arabic and English works operate within—the social, cultural, and political contexts, as well as the linguistic ones.

One of the very first issues that we confronted and continued to discuss from the first time we read the manuscript until we sent it off to the publisher was how to work with expressions that we knew would ring differently in the ears of Arabic and English readers. The most obvious examples are the words that we eventually would translate as "agent," "collaborator," and "collaborating agent." In the Arabic text, people who served these roles—mainly Lebanese people who worked with the Israeli military intelligence and military forces as part of the occupation of South Lebanon—are referred to in this way. Not only might this appear as an adjective used to describe these people or a noun describing what they did, but it is often used almost as a title preceding their name. In English this constant repetition of the word "agent" felt heavy on the text. Moreover, the words "agent" and "collaborator," though appropriate in this context, do not tend to be used as frequently in English in this way. Our solution to this challenge was to reduce the number of times these words were used in the translation. We did not use them as titles, either, as we deemed that it might make the text sound too foreign and too translated. However, we did choose to use the words more frequently than might have been done in a text originally written in English; we also varied between "agent," "collaborator," and "collaborating agent"— depending on the specific context. This made the text feel like it was written in the 1980s under Israeli occupation, while still allowing it to breathe a bit in English and take on an English-speaking life.

Though these words and expressions are the more obvious and challenging example of the time and place the text is set in, they are not the only elements that were tricky to translate. There are other words that lend the memoir the feel of being a work embodying the resistance. In these instances, we took care in deciding how to use specific words. The words "comrade" and "party comrade" are used throughout the text, as are the expressions "sister-prisoner" and "brother-prisoner." We contemplated words that would sound less dated and revolutionary, but in the end decided in favor of more direct translations. We felt that it was extremely important that the book retain its revolutionary tone of resistance, as well as its setting and context, and that it transport the reader back to the atmosphere of 1980s South Lebanon under Israeli occupation.

There were very few terms used in the Arabic memoir that we felt compelled to transliterate from the Arabic. We left the word "kilfa," which signifies the rotation of chores and duties carried out by prisoners, as is. One reason for this is that there is not a directly translatable one-word equivalent. Another is that it is not a common word in Arabic, either, and Nawal, the narrator, explains what it means in the text. We also incorporated the word "inshallah," meaning God willing, several times. We dealt with other religious expressions, like Qur'anic verses, by marking them as such, though they are simply dropped into the text in Arabic with no further elaboration. In the case of specific names or types of prayers, Nawal herself added these in footnotes which are retained. We were aware while translating that some elements of context might feel missing in English, but we did not extensively cushion the translation nor provide more explanations than were given in the Arabic original. One reason is that the Arabic memoir (Beirut, Aba'ad 2020) is published with extensive footnotes, as well as an introduction—both appear in the translation. We did not want to weigh down the translation by adding even more explanations.

We would like to also flag the use of footnotes in this text. All of the footnotes are in keeping with the original Arabic text, where it is noted if they were added by the author herself (NB) or the editors (MA and MH). As translators, we added a couple, which are marked as (MH and CN). The use of initials in the footnotes prompts us also to mention here the use of initials in the main text, used to protect identities rather than reveal them: Nawal refers to most of the other women in prison with her by their initials. We have directly transcribed these from the original text and assigned names that were marked by Arabic letters without an obvious English equivalent as follows: those beginning with 'ayn are represented by A and those with a hamza as I.

In one footnote we do explain one of Nawal's wordplays—on the name of the man she had planned to assassinate. Husayn Abdel-Nabi's surname is a compound word consisting of two parts in Arabic, Abdel, meaning "servant of," and Nabi, meaning "Prophet." This common name in Arabic thus means "Servant of the Prophet." Playing on this idea, she replaces the word Abdel with Aduw-el, meaning "enemy of," throughout most of the text. As such, his name would translate into "Enemy of the Prophet." In doing so, the author creates this person very much as the villain, which is of course the role he played in real life in the community where he lived and operated during the occupation of South Lebanon. She also utilizes this to emphasize that he was a traitor to his community, people, country, and religion. Because it is such an important and strong message, we wished to retain this wordplay and send an equally strong message in the translation, therefore rendering his name as "Enemy-Nabi," with a footnote. We hoped that we could achieve some effect in creating a strange-sounding name in English. We know it is not the same effect as the wordplay that any Arabic reader would immediately recognize but hope that by using a hybrid word and footnoting it, we would be sufficiently cushioning it for an English reader not to be alienated by the text but to seek out the information in the footnote—thereby glimpsing a bit inside the Arabic language of the text in the process.

We made another, somewhat opposite choice, in rendering an idea that is implied within the text less visible in the translation. Throughout the memoir—especially at the beginning when she is contemplating arrest and is first imprisoned in Khiam—Nawal thinks and talks a lot about the possibility of sexual assault or rape. The word she uses to render this in Arabic, however, is the more general word "assault" (الاعتداء). But it is obvious from context that she is referring to this more specific kind of assault, for example, when she has just suffered a beating by an interrogator and then wonders if she will be "assaulted." We debated between

166

ourselves if we should leave this subtlety and nuance in the text or bring it out and mark it more specifically. In the end, we opted to leave the implication as Nawal does in Arabic and allow readers to draw it out themselves. We hoped that by contextualizing this in the Introduction as well as in this translators' note, that the idea could be made clear and that Nawal's more indirect way of referring to this specific kind of attack would be implicitly understood.

There are many other parts of this translation that were challenging, including the use of songs, poems, and revolutionary chants which inevitably lose their power and layers of meaning when translated. We have rendered these as clearly as we could and provided the titles of songs and poems, as they can be found easily through a Google search, so a reader who would like to learn more can access them.

One final difficulty that came up in translation has to do with the use of pronouns: namely, the way Nawal sometimes abruptly switches from the first-person "I" to the second-person "you." Without trying to read too deeply into the reason she does so, we chose to simply mirror these switches in translation as they appear in the source text and trust the reader's intuition.

As translators we hope to have struck the appropriate balance in our choices to present Nawal Baidoun's memoir in a way that is accessible, while remaining true to its original form. We also hope that you find this work as moving and inspirational as we do.

Michelle Hartman and Caline Nasrallah
Montreal/ Beirut, November 2020

Nawal Baidoun with Andree Lahoud, president Emil Lahoud's wife
after the liberation of Khiam Prison

Nawal Baidoun with Hajj Abu Ali al-Dirani inside the Prison after its liberation

## — TRANSLATORS' AND EDITORS' ACKNOWLEDGMENTS —

Most importantly, our thanks are due to Nawal Baidoun for sharing her story with us, so that we in turn could share it with English-speaking readers. Your courage continues to inspire us, Nawal. Thanks also to those that led us to her, including Tawfiq al-Mansouri (Abu Wahid) and Sanaa Ali Ahmad. We extend our deepest appreciation to Nawal, Sanaa and all the other women who shared their stories of the Lebanese Civil War with us and contributed to the Women's War Stories project. We would like to acknowledge that this project has been funded in part by the Social Sciences and Humanities Research Council of Canada; we thank the Department of History and Classical Studies and the Institute of Islamic Studies at McGill University for their support as well. Our heartfelt thanks to Michel Moushabeck and his team at Interlink Publishing whose vision makes it possible for a memoir like this to see the light of day in English. The commitment to letting stories like Nawal's be heard is ever more important today.

To finish this project, we relied on the help of research assistants Ralph Haddad, Haneen Eldiri, and Sarah Abdelshamy. Sarah was a part of this project from the beginning and we would like to thank her for her creativity and dedicated work on it. We acknowledge Massoud Younes and Iman Humaydan for helping us secure a copy of the original manuscript, and Khalil Saghir of the Bint Jbayl website that first published some excerpts from it in Arabic. Nawal Baidoun's memoir appeared in Arabic in 2020 (Aba'ad, Beirut). The translators would like to specifically thank Hajar Assaad for her assistance in moving the text into English. We greatly appreciate her attention to detail and nuance which helped to smooth the translation and make it more readable in English.

Malek Abisaab, Michelle Hartman, and Caline Nasrallah

Nawal Baidoun with nuns

## ABOUT THE AUTHOR

**Nawal Baidoun** is a lifelong militant and activist from Bint Jbeil, South Lebanon. Before the occupation she graduated from law school; she subsequently worked as a teacher; and today is the Principal of the High School in Bint Jbeil. She is a founding and active member of the Lebanese Association for Prisoners and Liberators (LAPL). A firm advocate of freedom and liberation for all, Baidoun continues to be active in the struggle for prisoners' rights and other social justice causes in Lebanon and beyond. This memoir is her first published work.

## ABOUT THE EDITORS AND TRANSLATORS

**Michelle Hartman** is Professor of Arabic Literature and Director of the Institute of Islamic Studies, McGill University. She is also a literary translator from Arabic to English and has translated more than a dozen novels, short story collections, and other pieces by Arab women writers. Her most recent translations published by Interlink include, Shahla Ujayli's *Summer with the Enemy* and *A Sky So Close to Us*, Radwa Ashour's *The Journey*, and Jana Elhassan's *All the Women Inside Me*.

**Malek Abisaab** is Associate Professor at McGill University in the departments of History and Classical Studies and the Institute of Islamic Studies. A historian, his work focuses on gender, labor, Islamism, and the nation-state in the Middle East. His books include, *Militant Women of a Fragile Nation* (Syracuse UP, 2010) and (with Rula Jurdi Abisaab) *The Shiites of Lebanon: Modernism, Communism, and Hizbullah's Islamists* (Syracuse UP, 2017).

**Caline Nasrallah** is a Master's student at the Institute of Islamic Studies at McGill University, where her research focuses on language as a feminist tool. She also works as a translator, mostly from Arabic to English, and has an MA in Translation from the École de traducteurs et d'interprètes de Beyrouth (USJ).